ME AND MY BEST FRIEND

ME AND MY BEST FRIEND

Thirty Stories over Thirty Years

RON COX

ME AND MY BEST FRIEND
Thirty Stories over Thirty Years

Interior Layout and Design by Alice Briggs
Book Cover Design by Abigael Elliott

ISBNs:
979-8-89165-190-6 Paperback
979-8-89165-201-9 Hardback
979-8-89165-200-2 ebook

Published by:
Streamline Books
Kansas City, MO
streamlinebookspublishing.com

BACKGROUND

This book is a nonfiction account of real-life events over the past thirty years. In some cases, the names of the parties were modified to protect their identities (or their careers . . .). Although many federal, state, county, and local laws may have been broken, the intent was not to get anyone fired or injured significantly.

After several years of constant prodding from our families and friends, we have decided to unveil our top thirty stories.

The timeframe of these stories spans from 1993 to 2023. Most of them take place in the heart of small-town Missouri.

Early in 1993, four random strangers (two couples) moved into the same neighborhood on the same day, across the street from each other. Both couples had only been married less than two years, and neither had started their families yet. In hindsight, that was probably a good thing in the early years. Little did we know that the husbands and wives would eventually become best friends, traveling the world together, raising children together, and living the American dream in the heartland.

DEDICATION

A special thanks to our friends and family members who have supported us for the past thirty years.

Additionally, this book is dedicated to three of our closest friends and family members:

In loving memory of Jordan Swearngin (a contributor to chapter 29). Jordan was called home by our Father on September 6th, 2015, at the tender age of 22.

In loving memory of Richard "Dick" Sprague, Chris's dad, who was called home on July 15th, 2022, to be with our Father. Dick was often talked about and certainly in our thoughts throughout most of our expeditions. Dick was a contributor to chapters 4 and 9.

Last but certainly not least was one of our closest friends and avid golfer, Ted Strobach. Ted was called home to our Father on April 9th, 2012. Ted was not only a high school state champion golfer, but he was also a contributor to chapter 8.

Rest in peace, our friends and family.

CONTENTS

ME AND MY BEST FRIEND

CHAPTER ONE

CHIEFS HOME GAME: LET'S ROLL

THE YEAR WAS 1996, and I had just received devastating news regarding some ongoing health concerns. After months of labs, doctor appointments, and visits with specialist after specialist, I was diagnosed with Wilson's disease.

For those nonmedical people like me, Wilson's disease is a hereditary medical diagnosis with no cure. In the 1980s and '90s, it was considered terminal. The body of someone that has Wilson's does not have the ability to process copper, which can be found in many foods people consume every day as part of their normal diets. For example, shellfish, pork, cereal, mushrooms, and even chocolate have copper within them naturally. Without the ability to process the copper, your body finds alternative ways to deal with copper. It either relocates to the brain or liver. In my case, it was having a devastating impact on my liver.

To determine the overall level of copper absorption, biopsies were ordered. A biopsy is when they go through your skin and take tissue samples with a needle. This procedure is not done under anesthetic, only a local numbing agent. This was supposed to be an outpatient procedure with somewhat of a predictable outcome. However, like most other medical procedures that I have had done, this turned out to be anything but ordinary. To start off the domino effect of bad experiences during this procedure, the doctor began by placing the tissue samples in the petri dish with wet solution, only to find out that he needed to collect samples for both dry and wet solutions. Not all wet. So, I went back into the surgery room for round two. During the second procedure, the doctor hit a nerve inside my abdomen. I came off the table and had a lot to say to him, only to pass out from the pain. Then I developed phlebitis and was required to spend the rest of the weekend in the hospital. So much for an outpatient procedure and going home the same day.

That weekend was a home game for the Kansas City Chiefs, which is an event Chris and I wouldn't miss if we were lucky enough to score some tickets. Unfortunately, I was stuck in the hospital recovering from a botched outpatient procedure and dealing with an inflamed and borderline infection in the vein in my arm.

Chris visited me in the hospital the day before the game and understood how disappointed and upset I was. So, in Chris-like fashion, he decided to take matters into his own hands. He stopped by the hospital on Sunday morning and encouraged me to check myself out of the hospital. It seemed like a reasonable thing to do since I was already feeling better and well on my way to recovery. I asked to have the monitors and tubes disconnected by a nurse, but it didn't go over so well. However, since they were unable to legally detain me any longer, the staff relented and let me check myself out of the hospital.

After attending a long tailgate and most of the game, I began to slip back into not feeling so well again. Chris knew it wasn't going to end well for either one of us, so he did the right thing and took me back to the hospital. According to Chris, he slowed down to approximately five miles an hour as he encouraged me to jump out at the curb and check myself back into the hospital. As I walked back into the hospital, the nurse at the front desk was not impressed and just pointed toward my vacant room and told me that my room was still there. To add to my pain, she did give me the ole "I told you, you would be back, and you would regret your decision to act irresponsible today." Boy was she ever right. I ended up spending another two days in the hospital before getting discharged. Lesson learned. I would not encourage others to follow my lead on this one.

Perhaps the most disappointed person was Raquel. She still gets that look in her eye when the subject is brought up at family events and Chris and Carra are present. As Chris always says, "That's what best friends are for!"

CHAPTER TWO

NATIONAL CHAMPIONSHIP GAME: PUBLIC TRANSPORTATION

O N JANUARY 3, 2001, we were in Miami, Florida, to watch the University of Oklahoma play the in-state favorites, the Florida State Seminoles. First, let me point out that Chris and I had traveled to Miami without tickets to the National Championship. However, the power of prayer worked in our favor.

We arrived the day before the game and scouted the area but had zero luck getting tickets from a street vendor. It was an in-state game for FSU, so all the extra tickets were already purchased by FSU fans. I can't fail to mention that Oklahoma was a double-digit underdog and was facing quarterback Chris Weinke, the reigning Heisman Trophy winner. But the underdog defense forced Weinke to turn the football over three times and never showed FSU the endzone all night. To me, an Oklahoma Sooners fan, it was a once-in-a-lifetime performance by the OU defense—they made the media and Heisman voters rethink their decision. However, the OU defensive performance wasn't the only miracle performed on that day.

The morning of the big game, Chris managed to pull off the first miracle of the day. During a casual breakfast encounter in a streetside café, Chris secured two lower-level tickets from two wonderful grandparents at face value. Apparently, they were OU season ticket holders and were randomly selected by OU Athletics in a drawing to get two lower-level tickets. However, they were not notified they had won until a week before kickoff. In the meantime, their kids had purchased two awesome lower-level tickets and surprised them a week earlier for their anniversary. Chris noticed the tickets lying on the table in front of the couple, softly approached, and said, "You must be OU fans. I see you're lucky enough to be going to the game." They said yes, and for some unknown reason, Chris asked, "Do you happen to have two extra tickets?"

We were so excited, but we now had to focus on next steps: transportation to the game, tailgating, and so on. That is where the next—and perhaps the most impactful—miracle occurred.

We approached the concierge station in the lobby of our hotel. This trip was not previously planned, so we were on a fixed budget, but come on, who knows if or when your favorite college team will ever play for a National Championship? Our hotel wasn't necessarily in the best part of Miami, nor did we have the resources to rent an appropriate tailgate-quality vehicle. Honestly, I was surprised they even had a concierge desk in our hotel. When we asked how far it was to Pro Player Stadium, and more importantly, how to get there, the concierge simply laughed. He said, "You have a couple options, and neither one is good. Take a cab, or go to the corner and wait for the public transit bus. It picks people up on the corner and takes them toward the stadium for work, but I'm not sure how close you'll get." Apparently, our hotel was across downtown from the game. After a short period of time to discern, we voted for the bus.

This is where the hard work started. As instructed, we reported to the corner intersection three hours before the kickoff. The good news was that the bus was nearly empty, with less than ten passengers. The bad news was that the driver, who was another young professional, said his last stop was still approximately half a mile from the stadium. Chris and I had arranged ourselves in the seat directly behind the driver in hopes of convincing him to take us all the way to the stadium.

Within a couple of blocks, the driver began to complain about his job, the company, and the fact he was already looking for another job. Perfect scenario for us! We took that opportunity to ask if he knew of any liquor stores along his route. The thing about the less-than-desirable neighborhood we rented our hotel in was that there were plenty of options. We asked the driver (to avoid anyone getting into further trouble, we will call him Truman) if he would stop at the next liquor store for a second so we could get some beer for our tailgate. We told him if he did, we would get him and the other ten riders something as well. Reluctantly, he conceded when the overwhelming number of riders agreed to a bottle of their favorite spirits. Chris and I nearly bought the entire store out of Mad Dog 20/20, big bottles of Colt 45, our favorite vodka bottle, and Budweiser, of course.

When we made it back to the bus with all the inventory, you would have thought we hit a big scratcher ticket. Chris started down the aisle, handing out bottles, and eight of the ten people seemed pleased. The remaining two didn't seem as impressed as we were. Perhaps the most concerning part was when the driver did a toast to Chris and me before he took a hit on the bottle. (Please note, this was way before camera technology was fully developed and even implemented.)

After all that we had been through that day, Truman decided the last half mile of the journey wasn't that far away, and he was probably going to either quit or get fired when the calls started coming in, so he took us to the gate at the stadium. After another toast, we were off to the game, and he was on his way.

Chris and I had arrived at the stadium for our game about two hours before kickoff. Epic!

CHAPTER THREE

2000 ORANGE BOWL: THE FLIGHT

O BVIOUSLY IF YOU completed reading Chapter Two, you already know that Chris and I made it to Orlando and eventually secured two awesome tickets to the National Championship game. But we nearly missed that opportunity because we nearly missed a connecting flight from St. Louis to Orlando.

Let me first say that making last-minute travel plans to a destination city where the NCAA College Football National Championship game is scheduled at the same time you are trying to go low-cost is a failed plan from the start. These types of plans are generally made while under the influence at a local sports bar. They seem rational at the time, but when you really sober up and have time to think, it's a bad idea nearly every time.

Through his place of business, Chris and his "connections" had "a gal" who was connected to a family that worked for Trans World Airlines, better known as TWA. You probably haven't heard of this airline, unless you are an older person like me. This is because they are no longer in business. I know what you're thinking: it's because of what I am about to tell you. But don't even go there. Our actions have nothing to do with them being out of business. At least, I don't think they are related. However, after reading this chapter, you may think there is a definite correlation.

The first leg of the flight from Kansas City to St. Louis was normal. The Kansas City airport is small and doesn't have a lot of flights. We had standby tickets, which Chris secured via his colleague at work. I was much younger back then and certainly not a seasoned traveler. I thought getting a standby ticket would give us nearly free flights. Well, it wasn't quite as easy as I originally thought. Fortunately, from Kansas City to St. Louis, the plane was only half full. Again, perhaps the airline going out of business may be related to the fact that some of their flights were only half full. I failed to mention previously that TWA was headquartered out of Kansas City. You would have thought they would dominate the air travel world out of their home turf.

Going from St. Louis with a standby ticket to Orlando was a much different challenge. Chris and I arrived in St. Louis a couple of hours before the flight was scheduled to go to Orlando. We approached the gate and there were two counter employees. The older employee—let's call her Karen—was rude, and we could tell already that she hated her job before we showed up. Her younger counterpart was approximately in her twenties. She was very pleasant and had not worked at TWA long enough to know how bad of an employee Karen was. Chris approached cautiously and asked Karen if we could get a seat on the flight to Orlando.

"*No*, it's already full," Karen said, loudly.

Chris responded, "Is there a standby list that we can place our names on in case other flights are delayed and don't arrive in St. Louis on time?"

She replied with a curt "Not going to happen" and reluctantly handed us off to her colleague, Amanda. Amanda took our names and told us she would do everything she could. Her attitude was much more pleasant. It may have had something to do with the cash I saw Chris place in her hand as a tip for at least giving it her best. Little did we know our luck was about to change over the next couple of hours.

As the boarding time approached, Karen started assisting some elderly passengers with wheelchairs onto the plane, all the while complaining that "the guys" never showed up to provide wheelchair assistance. That was the window that opened for us. We approached the counter again, and Amanda said, "You might be in luck: there's a plane that was stuck in Boston and will be arriving later that has four passengers on it. I'll try to help you." Chris once again applied his magical charm and slid another twenty to help her process our passes quicker.

Karen came back off the plane and said, "I have one more passenger to assist and then I'm heading to the restroom. I've been standing here for two hours. Please start boarding the plane and dismiss the two standby passengers. We won't be able to accommodate them this time."

Chris and I were so upset that Karen wasn't willing to let us get on the flight since Amanda had already let the cat out of the bag and told us about the delayed Boston flight. We didn't want to start a fight, so we simply sat in the front row at the terminal gate, making eye contact with Amanda every chance we got. Eventually, Karen stepped off the plane for the last time and went on her potty run. Amanda motioned to Chris and me to approach the counter.

"Now is your chance," she whispered. "Go on the plane and find an open seat. Everyone else that's here should already be on the plane."

So, we simply walked down the jetway and acted like we actually had a ticket. We boarded the plane, and luckily for us there were two open seats in the second-to-last row, well out of everyone's way. We gave each other a high five and sat quietly waiting for takeoff. However, we were not out of the weeds yet. A couple minutes after taking our seats, we noticed Karen coming down the aisle with a seat roster, looking at people.

"If we're going to stay on this flight, you need to grab that barf bag and bury your face in it," Chris said. "Now our fate is in God's hands."

When Karen was near row 12, which was about twenty rows ahead of us, the captain came on the PA system and said, "We have been cleared for departure. Please take your seats and fasten your belts for an on-time departure." Apparently, that is exactly what we needed. Back then, union pilots got bonuses based on their on-time departures and arrivals. With that announcement, Karen turned around and left the plane.

That was a huge win for us. We actually got onto an airplane (albeit before 9/11) without a ticket or seat assignment. We were so excited that we started drinking during the announcements provided by the flight attendants.

We were not aware that TWA had a two-drink-per-passenger policy, but we found out before our plane left Missouri airspace. The flight attendant came by and said, "I'm sorry, but you two have already received a drink and a shot. I'm not allowed to give you anymore." Chris asked if she could give us someone else's quota of drinks. She at least had a sense of humor and laughed at him as she said, "No." Chris, being the genius that he is, found out that cash was king and TWA policies were only suggestions. Keep in mind, we were roughly in row 34 of a thirty-five-row plane. People around us showed up drunk and didn't even care. So, Chris started dropping five-dollar bills on the floor and throwing them back toward the flight attendant's working area. Ms. Flight Attendant graciously smiled and started making it rain airplane bottles of vodka and an occasional coke to help keep us awake during the long flight. Somehow, we managed to make it to Orlando and ground transportation got us to the hotel safely from what I was told. Despite Karen's repeated attempts to not provide good customer service and help us get to the National Championship, we made it to Orlando.

CHAPTER FOUR

2007 FIESTA BOWL: THE IDAHO HOT POTATO GAME

THE GAME WAS played on New Year's Day, 2007, in Glendale, Arizona, at the University of Phoenix stadium. The game was going to be an epic battle: Boise State had won every regular season game and supported a 12–0 record, while the Sooners had a great season as well, with an 11–2 record.

The Boise State Broncos came to play and prove to the world that they belonged in a BCS bowl game despite being from a much smaller conference. They got off to a great start and took a commanding 21–10 lead by the end of the first half. The Broncos managed to hold the eleven-point advantage even through the third quarter. Heading into the final quarter, the Sooners needed to make up some ground. Oklahoma took advantage of a poor throw by the Broncos quarterback and took it back for a pick six late in the quarter to take the lead. However, the Broncos didn't give up. With some luck and the old hook and ladder trick play, the Broncos scored late to tie up the game in the fourth quarter.

Heading into overtime, the game was up for grabs. The Sooners got the ball first, and future NFL running back Adrian Peterson took it to the house for a touchdown. After the extra point, the Sooners were up seven points. Now it was the Broncos' possession on offense. They too would end up scoring a touchdown. After a lengthy timeout by the coach, Chris Petersen, the Broncos decided to go for a two-point conversion to end the game and not allow the Sooners back on the field. The thought of going for a two-point conversion at this time was unbelievable. However, I believe Coach Petersen knew that the longer the Sooners stayed around, the higher the chances would be that it wouldn't end well for the Broncos.

In a split second, the Broncos quarterback ran an old-school play from the elementary school playground. Back in the day we affectionately called it the "Statue of Liberty" because the quarterback literally stands in the pocket poised like the Statue of Liberty, drawing attention to himself while the person behind him sneaks the ball from behind his waist and runs for the corner of the endzone as fast as possible. The play fooled the Sooners, and the two-point conversation was successful. The game was now over.

To this day, many sports broadcasters will tell you this was the greatest BCS game ever played. Coming down to overtime, the last play was pulled from an elementary school playground. *Wow*!

Outside of the epic game, however, perhaps the biggest surprise play was not to happen until the next day.

Chris and I decided to stay in Arizona and spend some quality time with Chris's father, Richard Sprague, a.k.a. "Dick," who lived in a nicely developed, master-planned community with several nice golf courses and a clubhouse in a nearby suburb of Phoenix. Dick knew that both of us were still trying to digest the twenty-four

Bud Lights and the last-minute loss by the Broncos from the night before. He asked if he could host us at his local country club and meet some of his closest friends and favorite waiters and staff. We enthusiastically agreed to go out with family and friends and just celebrate the love shared among everyone. Of course, neither of us were going to say no to some Tito's and a nice steak dinner.

One major problem suddenly appeared from across the restaurant. A large family was sitting together enjoying their steak and seafood and, of course, Idaho potatoes. In a sign of gratitude or poor sportsmanship, the tribal elder decided to bring over a token and present it to Chris. It didn't take long for us to recognize their Boise State shirts, as Chris and I were still proudly wearing our Sooner apparel. Suddenly, Chris pressed his fork deep into the Idaho potato and firmly launched it across the restaurant with precision accuracy. It landed directly in the middle of the family's table, where it slid to a rest after knocking over several waters and a wine glass or two. Chris stood up and said, "Thank you for the potato, but with all due respect, nothing good has ever come from Idaho—not even their potatoes."

The older gentleman was at a loss for words and simply walked back across the restaurant and began to pick up the mess. To everyone's surprise, we weren't asked to leave and were able to enjoy the rest of our meal. I wasn't sure who was more upset: the restaurant manager, or Dick. Either way, nothing was hurt by the potato other than feelings.

CHAPTER FIVE

OKLAHOMA VERSUS TEXAS: THE TAXI DRIVER

I N 2011, W E took a trip to Dallas, Texas, to watch the top two football teams from the Big 12 Conference, the Texas Longhorns versus our Oklahoma Sooners. The history of this game is one of the best and biggest rivalries in college football. Unfortunately (or fortunately, depending on which team you root for), the venue tends to be a home game each year for Texas. However, to be fair, neither team has hosted this game at their own stadium for years. In fact, the teams first played each other in 1900 in Austin, Texas. At the time of this writing, the overall record in the 119 games played is 63–51–5, with Texas holding the advantage. Over the years, the sports writers have renamed the annual game as the "Red River Rivalry" because of the programs' relationship geographically. The setting is also iconic as it takes place in the Cotton Bowl stadium, located right in the center of the country's largest state fair (Texas). The game was amazing if you are a Sooners fan. They ended up "hanging a fifty" on the Longhorns that day in a blowout.

But this story isn't about the game—it's about what happened the day before. Similar to one of our previous stories, especially the one about Orlando, Florida, this story is more about transportation. For some reason, Chris and I do not have the best of luck when it comes to getting to and from big games. The trip to Dallas was no different. Some of the misunderstandings tend to be a result of, as Chris would say, "being overserved." (I'll refer to Chris and I saying "overserved" many other times throughout the rest of this book; to be clear, we mean it in a tongue-in-cheek way.)

The day before the Red River Rivalry, we arrived at Love Field in Dallas, Texas, in the early evening and headed straight to the hotel to check in before heading to the West End to join our fellow fans to tailgate. Obviously, we were excited, the Southwest flight was on time, and everything was going great. Then we ran into an unethical cab driver. We provided him with our hotel address, and it was anticipated according to GPS that we would arrive in fifteen to twenty minutes. As we approached our exit from the highway, we noticed the driver didn't merge onto the exit ramp but continued to go down the highway. The next offramp was two-and-a-half miles away. He apologized and we did the five miles down and back. The second time the driver approached our off-ramp, he continued on again and missed the exit for a second time.

This time, Chris and I were beginning to get argumentative with him. Unfortunately, we were not aware if he could understand us: his English was very broken, and he just smiled and laughed and said something that sounded like "my bad." After going another five miles round trip, we approached the hotel off-ramp for a third time. The ironic thing is that the hotel was sitting right at that intersection, and we could have walked a couple hundred feet to the large parking lot. The driver started to miss the turn yet again, and Chris lunged forward and told the driver to pull over on the side of the highway off-ramp. When the car came to a stop, Chris jumped out and told the driver to pop the trunk. I was still sitting inside the cab in the back seat, on the passenger side. I was the lucky one—I wasn't standing near the seventy-mile-an-hour traffic like Chris. The driver popped the trunk, and Chris grabbed both small bags. I wasn't quite sure what was going on, but I knew I should respect Chris's decision to walk the remaining hundred yards.

As I exited the cab, I noticed the meter read forty-seven dollars. Chris walked next to the driver's window and threw a twenty-dollar bill into the window and told the cab driver to keep the change and "shut the f*** up." Looking through the passenger window, I noticed the driver was reaching under his seat, I assume for his weapon to threaten us or to just shoot Chris. Without missing a beat, Chris handed me my bag and said, "Let's walk the rest of the way. We're already thirty minutes late because of this idiot and I need a drink."

I thought I was going to die on the side of the highway that night. The good news is that the cab driver just took off and drove down the highway. We lived to tell that story and go watch the game the next day.

CHAPTER SIX

RED RIVER RIVALRY: DRY COUNTY

OCTOBER IS THE perfect time of the year to host the Texas Fair, one of the largest in the United States. Although many states host their annual state fairs in the summer when kids are out of school, it's simply way too hot and humid in Texas in July or August, in my opinion.

Back in the 1990s and early 2000s, there were still many dry counties in the state of Texas (google it if you don't believe me). This is an important fact that everyone needs to know when planning travel to Texas for a football game, especially when pregame activities like tailgating are involved.

Chris and I checked into the hotel late afternoon on the day before the big game with our families. By now, we had two children each. Everyone was excited to go to the Texas State Fair the next morning, but Chris and I were excited to for an entirely different reason. Although we knew the 4-H animal petting zoo and carnival rides were important to our wives and kids, we wanted to watch the big game.

After unpacking, Chris and I proceeded to the front desk to ask about directions to the local liquor store to get drinks for the pool and tailgate the next day. This is when we learned for the first time about dry counties.

"No worries," the person at the front desk said. "There's an old converted Amoco gas station a couple miles down the highway once you cross over into the next county."

Equipped with this knowledge and directions, we set out to pick up the drinks for ourselves and our wives. It was about fifteen minutes from the hotel, which wasn't too bad. So off we went on this life-changing event.

As we approached the converted gas station where the gas pumps had been removed, we saw cars lined up out front. This looked sketchy on many levels. I noticed once we pulled off the highway that the neighborhood wasn't exactly the best. The minivan we drove really started to stand out. If you know me at all, you know that I am not the most patient person in the world. In fact, Chris might say I am the least patient person he knows. Placing me and my best friend in a bad neighborhood only added to the anxiety. At one point, I even said, "Perhaps we should stop drinking."

Obviously, Chris said, "That's not an option."

We watched and found out the line of cars and trucks would pull up to where there was once a gas pump. Someone would come out from inside the building and take the orders and go back inside and bring out the order. Similar to a fast-food restaurant. Well, this was taking way too long, so I pulled over next to the building and parked. Chris mentioned that he would stay in the van and make sure no one stole it. Did I mention there were about ten homeless people sitting up against the wall of the old gas station?

I walked into the side entrance of the dimly lit gas station and a very large man placed a shotgun to my temple and said, "Who the f*** do you think you are?" After a short pause to control my bowels, I responded that I was just trying to purchase some beer. The guy responded, "Go back to your f****** van and get back in line like everyone else."

Realizing that I was not shot and still alive, I responded, "I have a wife and kids waiting for me back at the hotel and just needed to hurry before she starts cussing at me again. I'll pay twice as much to you in cash to make it happen." Remember from the previous chapters: cash is king.

The big guy found it hard to say no to cash, so he shouted to a young girl running to and from the beer cooler, "Get this man a suitcase of Bud Light." He put the gun down and I handed him two twenties and walked out.

As I approached the van, I noticed Chris had cracked the window about six inches and was flipping coins out of it to several people who were picking them up in the parking stall

next to the van. I asked Chris what the hell he was doing. He responded, "They kept coming up to the van and tapping on the window and asking for money. I was nervous so I started flipping coins out of the window to them. Thank goodness you had a lot of change in your console."

As strange as that seemed at the time, I was just glad to still be alive.

When I told Chris about the shotgun to the temple, he couldn't believe he missed all that while he was handing out coins.

Back at the hotel, the wives were not impressed. But they did help us finish off the suitcase of Bud Light.

CHAPTER SEVEN

BIG 12 BASKETBALL TOURNAMENT IN KANSAS CITY: WHERE ARE WE?

CHRIS AND I are best friends. We have spent three decades together raising four children and trying to not let our wives know that we have both married up. Given that our wives are also best friends and all four of our children are extremely close, the children even get labeled as cousins, and all four parents are affectionately called aunt and uncle. Because of these close relationships, we always find ourselves doing a lot together, especially going to sporting events. Whether it be with all the family members, the wives, or just Chris and I, we have always enjoyed watching games together. It also helps that we like the same sports and teams.

In the 1990s, the Big 12 basketball tournament was consistently hosted in Kansas City, the heart of Big 12 country.

The men's tournament was always played near downtown at Kemper Arena. Most will tell you that the arena wasn't located in the best part of town, but it had a ton of history and a lot of adjacent parking lots from the old stockyard days at the turn of the century. Unfortunately, it wasn't close to an entertainment area, and there were very few available restaurants or bars. The best I can remember is less than five. Most fans had to adjust to tailgates at pop-up tents or parking lot stalls and bring their own beer. This wasn't ideal, but you always made new friends in the parking lot or while waiting in the long lines to hit the port-a-potties that were in the surrounding parking lots and on the islands.

The tournament format was also different than most are used to. You'd get a "pass or session" ticket to watch two games before they would kick everyone out of the arena into the parking lot, only to reopen and let people in a couple of hours later for the second session. Typically, there was a late morning and early afternoon game, then a late afternoon and early evening game. In my opinion, this is dangerous for fans who like to tailgate and drink. To help provide something to do, some local gentlemen's clubs would have free drink coupons and offer shuttles to and from to go watch the girls dance between sessions. Heck, I've heard stories that some fans never made it back to watch their own college because the club show was better than their basketball team.

It was a Friday, and Chris and I were excited because we managed to get tickets for both sessions that day. To be able to afford both sessions, we purchased tickets that were in the top row of the arena. The morning started off with a healthy breakfast buffet in the downtown area about thirty minutes from the arena. We had a morning toast with the standard Bloody Marys, then headed over for the first session. According to eyewitnesses and some pieced-together memories between Chris and I, the party continued from the Blood Mary bar throughout the first session to several mixed drinks afterward. We did not pace ourselves and were probably overserved by the end of the first game in the first session. However, we persevered and ordered more drinks as the second game of the first session tipped off. By half time of the second game, we decided we should take a nap to rest up for the evening session. The game wasn't close, and neither one of our teams was playing in the second game anyway.

Some might ask, "Did you both take a nap or pass out?" Back then, I'm not sure we knew the difference. Either way, the session apparently ended, and the arena had been one hundred percent cleared out when a young arena staff member kindly stopped by, tapped Chris on the shoulder, and said, "Sir, you and your friend must leave the arena. We've cleared everyone else out and have cleaned up all the trash. The fans with the second session tickets will be coming in in the next half hour."

Apparently, this "nap" had lasted a couple of hours, and neither one of us knew what had actually happened. After leaving the arena and heading back to the parking lot, we proceeded to slam some bottles of water plus a couple of beers, then went back in for session two. What an eventful Friday.

CHAPTER EIGHT

CHARITY GOLF TOURNAMENT: WHERE IS TED? & WHERE DID THOSE FLOWERS COME FROM?

CHRIS AND I are both givers. We are selfless when it comes to giving our time, talent, and treasure to organizations our families feel passionate about. One of those special events and opportunities to give back presented itself in Kansas City when I was asked to sponsor a foursome for a local golf tournament to recognize and remember fallen first responders. The event was held over the summer at one of the most prestigious and historic courses near downtown Kansas City. I reached out and asked a couple of friends to join Chris and I for the event. When they found out what the event was about and who it would benefit, they agreed to participate.

It's worth noting that Chris and I are very average golfers, and most would describe us as weekend hackers. But we do like to play (and more importantly, just have fun). The two guest players that I invited for this event were much more experienced and took the tournaments more seriously. However, the foursome did have something in common: we all liked to drink while playing golf.

The tournament kicked off just after lunch, so it was hot, and a lot of beverages would be needed to get through the first round just to stay hydrated. We did our best to keep up. We loaded the cart with beer and bottled water, as did our partners, Ted and Mark, with their cart. Then we stopped by the patio to listen to the instructions for the event as well as a word from the sponsors. A former veteran also spoke about the purpose of the event. We purchased some raffle tickets for various items, including sports memorabilia, four single-game tickets to the Kansas City Chiefs, and a chance to win two season tickets to the Kansas City Royals. Let's face it: in the 1990s, they were giving away Royals tickets, but it was still a fun experience for kids.

As we finished the front nine, we were playing well for two rookies and two dedicated partners. Chris and I headed toward the clubhouse for a quick restroom break and to reload the cooler. This is where another one of those "Chris-and-Ron moments" happened. For some unknown reason, I was the driver of the golf cart. Short straw, possibly. I was carrying on a conversation with Chris and was probably already somewhat overserved by Chris, Mark, or Ted. Nonetheless, I veered off the cart path as we approached the big patio and ended up hitting a very large whiskey barrel full of beautiful plants and flowers. The impact knocked the planter a few feet, making a very loud noise, and broke the axle on the golf cart. Apparently, the noise was so loud on impact that Chris noticed several of the older golfers practicing on the putting green jump and began to run away. Both of us flew out of the golf cart and onto the patio.

A couple of minutes later, a young gentleman approached from the side of the clubhouse where you typically return your carts. He asked what happened, and so I explained that the axle broke, which was a completely honest assessment. However, what the young fellow didn't ask (thank goodness) was if the cart broke before or after impact. The employee was very apologetic and brought us another cart while we took our bathroom break and reloaded. When we walked back out of the clubhouse, our clubs were already switched and our cooler was fully stocked. Chris and I survived the crash with only a couple of scratches. Off we went to meet Ted and Mark on the back nine. When we arrived, they asked about the delay, and we explained it was a long restroom break, and oh, the axle broke on the golf cart. No big deal.

This wasn't the craziest thing of the day, although it could have ended much worse. With only three holes left in the tournament, Ted began to fall asleep (or pass out) in the cart, and we had a hard time getting him up to take his shot. With two holes left, we needed a long putt to save a birdie on the hole. All three of us missed, and we needed Ted to wake up and take his shot.

Throughout the day, Ted was the best putter on our team despite being way overserved. He hit several long attempts when he was sober. When I tapped him on his shoulder, he asked where we were and why I had to wake him up. So, I had to explain that we were still playing golf with two holes left and that we might actually win the tournament if he could hit a twenty-five-foot-long putt. Ted said, "No problem."

I helped Ted out of the golf cart. He walked over to the edge of the green and stopped, lit a cigarette, gauged the angle, and abruptly addressed the putt. To our surprise, he hit it. A once-in-a-lifetime putt. After we celebrated the miracle, Ted said he was walking to the parking lot to throw up. He told us to go ahead and play the last hole without him. The seventeenth hole was close to the parking lot, so we supported his plan. We finished the eighteenth hole, turned in our carts, and went to see if we won the tournament. Just our luck, we took second place by a single stroke. Then they drew the three winning tickets from the box. The first one was a signed football—no such luck. The next one was the Chiefs single-game tickets. Again, no such luck. The last drawing was the two season tickets to the Royals. Chris, Mark, Ted, and I had all bought our tickets back-to-back, so they were only different by one digit. I was 1020, Chris was 1021, Ted was 1022, and Mark was 1023. They announced the winner: 1022. But there was a problem: you needed to be present to win. I shouted out, "Our teammate is 1022, but he's in the parking lot putting away his clubs! Give us a minute to get him and the ticket."

The three of us headed to the parking lot but could not locate Ted within a couple of minutes, so they pulled another winner. After twenty-plus minutes, we found Ted somewhere between the seventeenth hole and parking lot in a small grove of trees, sleeping. By the way, Ted was a big Royals fan.

CHAPTER NINE

ANNUAL ARIZONA GOLF TRIP AND FAMILY REUNION: ARE YOU A LICENSED THERAPIST? & THE JUMPING CACTUS

THE SPRAGUE FAMILY went above and beyond when it came to their annual family reunion. They held it in beautiful Scottsdale, Arizona, hosted by Chris's father. It was a long weekend event, where they hosted friends and neighbors as well. Almost everyone there liked to play golf, hang out by the pool, and drink. From time to time, these family reunions could and often did get somewhat out of hand. Some would say that's because they were held in August, and the heat gets to your brain in the dry desert. The first time I attended one of these reunions, after some convincing from Chris, little did I know that the weekend would end with my blood being shed, three potential felonies, and more.

Let's start with the first day in Arizona. It was a normal August day in the desert: hotter than crap. Chris and I set out to break the longstanding outdoor hot tub record for the state. We managed to stay in the hot tub at Señor Sprague's casa for roughly four straight hours. Don't ask about the pee breaks, or lack thereof—we're still trying to find the answer to that question.

The gracious host, Señor Sprague (as Chris often referred to him), did his best to supply beer and hard liquor until we emptied the outdoor and indoor liquor cabinets. Once we ran out of booze, it was time to get out and get dressed for our dinner reservations. Upon our return from a wonderful dinner with friends and family, we headed back to the patio for a nice stiff drink and cigars. One thing that Chris forgot to share with me before the trip was the fact that his stepmother once won a national championship in the Arizona amateur division for rolling and moisturizing a cigar just using her mouth and tongue. I'm not sure who was more surprised with her technique: Chris, or me. Either way, after the shock and awe settled, we smoked and drank the evening away.

The next day was the big event: tournament day at the course. Señor Sprague was appropriately paired with his best friend, Dr. Fran, the dentist. Chris and I were also paired together to complete the group of four.

The rules of the tournament were very simple: both players from the same cart get to hit a ball, and you play the best shot of the two. Well, Señor Sprague hit a nice shot down the center of the fairway, and likewise, I hit a nice shot down the center. Neither Chris nor Fran was as lucky. They hit shots in the rough, so Fran went to retrieve his ball, and I told Chris I would walk over and pick up his ball while he and Señor Sprague drove down the middle of the fairway to find the two balls we wanted to play. I noticed a golf ball first, and approached the rough to pick it up, not knowing if it was Fran's or Chris's golf ball. As I bent over to pick up the ball, a jumping cholla a foot behind me latched onto my butt. As I jumped, the entire branch tore away from the trunk of the cactus and got stuck on my shorts. Fran was only a few feet away and came over to help. He attempted to surgically remove the branch from my behind with two golf clubs. Keep in mind, Fran is a dentist and does surgery all the time. Well, it didn't work out as well this time. The branch became dislodged from my butt region and firmly planted itself onto Fran's chest.

I took the same clubs Fran used and began to remove the branch from Fran's chest. Luckily, I was able to get it removed from Fran with no further issues. Now, both of us were bleeding as we walked to the center of the fairway to meet up with Señor Sprague and Chris. They had heard the yelling and screaming but had no idea what was happening. The entire event took less than two minutes but had a lifelong impact. Fran now wore a bloody shirt, and I had bloody shorts to match for the remainder of the seventeen holes. None of us had even heard of attacking cactuses before this happened. I'm not sure who got the worst of it: Fran, or me. I don't think I'll be offering to go look for Chris's golf balls in the future.

The next day we played another epic round of golf. We had played three rounds of golf in two days, so our bodies were definitely hurting and sore. On the final day, to end a tremendous weekend and a long day of golfing, we decided to stop on the way home for a nice steak dinner. Señor Sprague knew the area well and suggested a steak house close to where he lived. This is where the three felonies nearly occurred.

I sat at the end of the table next to the oldest players, Señor Sprague and Dr. Fran. After we ordered our cocktails, some middle-aged Hispanic servers approached me, Señor Sprague, and Dr. Fran to see what appetizers we wanted. Not missing a beat, doc Fran and Señor Sprague ordered a seafood tower and about every other expensive appetizer they could find. Perhaps doc Fran and I were just happy to still be alive. One server took notice and kept trying to upsell the older guys. A few minutes later, that server showed back up with two other Hispanic server friends, asking if we all needed back massages after a long three rounds of golf. The older of the three Hispanic servers said she was a "professional," and the three of them smiled and laughed. I perked up and started paying more attention to the conversation. I had my doubts about her honesty and credentials as a professional therapist. About ten minutes later, the food arrived, and the server let us know that she had three "therapists" lined up to come over after dinner to our place and give us all "massages" for one hundred dollars each if all six of us agreed. Señor Sprague told her he thought that was a good deal. He would let her know after dinner.

I knew something was up and quickly asked Chris to go to the restroom for a quick piss and conversation. In the restroom I told Chris that he needed to talk to his father. He was unknowingly ordering three Hispanic hookers that were servers on the side to come back to our place after dinner for "massages." Chris was unaware of the conversation, so he went back to the table and asked his dad to step outside for a short meeting with the two of us. Once we explained in more detail that our servers were not licensed or trained massage therapists and that they had lied, he was somewhat embarrassed and asked for forgiveness for being so naïve.

Señor went back inside and respectfully declined the "massage therapy." Thank goodness none of us got sick from the servers doing something to our food. The steak and seafood were outstanding, and no one got arrested for soliciting prostitutes.

CHAPTER TEN

HILTON HEAD ISLAND FAMILY VACATION: WE ARE NOT SHARK FISHING

WHEN THE SPRAGUE and Cox family children were younger, both families frequently traveled to Hilton Head Island, South Carolina, to hang out on the white-sand beaches, swim, set crab pots, and fish from the surf. It was an amazing time on the island for summer vacations. The summer this next story comes from was no different. The weather was beautiful, the children were pulling in crab pots with blue crabs, and the fishing rods were getting a lot of bites.

One morning I decided that I wanted to get up early and go fishing by myself for some much-needed peace and quiet. Just me and the waves. "Ass in the sand, toes in the water." It was a typical beautiful sunrise, and the tide was low. Before me were miles and miles of open beach and calm waves. I got my line

41

cast out in the surf, settled along the beach for a morning Bloody Mary, and within a couple of minutes, here comes a young family: a mom and two small children. Sure enough, with miles of open beach with not a soul in sight, she settles within ten yards of me and my fishing pole.

A few minutes later, the little boy about seven years old hit the open water first and waded out to his knees. Following behind was his younger sister, about four years old. The mom settled back into a chair and started reading a book. I kept a watchful eye on the fishing pole and line to ensure the younger children were not going to cross the line or get caught up. Not exactly what I was looking for when I headed to the beach. About a half hour later, I had my first bite. I caught a small shark about two feet long. Once I landed the shark on the beach, the brother and sister walked over with excitement and curiosity and asked, "What kind of fish is it?"

Not missing a beat or really thinking about it, I told them that it was a shark. The little boy was amazed. They both asked if they could feel the shark. The skin on a shark is very rough, like sandpaper. They thought that was super cool. A couple of minutes later, their mom decided to put her book down and walk over to inspect and to see if she could get a picture of the fish with her two children. She had an Eastern European accent and asked what type of fish it was. Again, I responded that it was a shark. She looked somewhat shocked and asked, "You caught that right there in front of us in the shallow water?"

"Yes," I responded, "and yesterday we caught about fifty. Some were even larger."

The young mother freaked out and told the children to get their stuff and all three left the beach after being there less than forty-five minutes. She seemed both upset and scared. Honestly, I couldn't believe that she really didn't expect there to be sharks in the ocean off the coast of Hilton Head Island. Either way, I was excited to once again be fishing without anyone around. As fishing continued, I caught several redfish, whiting, and other species that were not identified.

A little bit later, Chris and the boys showed up to fish and brought drinks. The bites continued to be good. That's when things got somewhat crazy. Chris and I decided to wade out farther into the surf and fish in the deeper water in hopes of catching larger fish. A few minutes later, Chris looked over his shoulder and noticed a fish and game agent was sitting in his pickup watching us from a distance. Within approximately ten minutes, he decided to drive his pickup down next to the water. As he got out of his truck, we could tell he was probably a college summer intern trying to make a couple bucks. He stood there for a while and didn't say anything. It was starting to get a little creepy. Finally, Chris lost his bait and started walking toward the shore to reload, and that's when the agent asked if we had fishing licenses. We responded affirmatively. He then said, "What bait are you using?" in an aggressive and smart-ass tone. I responded that we were using shrimp and squid from the local marina. The young agent then let us know that they received a call at the local office from a woman stating that a guy was fishing for shark from the beach. Then he said, "You know it's illegal to fish from the shore for sharks. You should not be catching shark."

I had already had enough from the young smart-ass agent, so I responded in my own smart-ass tone, "Has anyone informed the shark to *not* bite on the rods and bait provided by the marina to the locals that are encouraged to fish from the shore? It seems to me like there might be a breakdown in communication with the local fish population and the fishermen. Over the past four days we've caught everything from stingrays to sharks, but fortunately no dolphins. How can we prevent the sharks from biting?"

Appearing somewhat disappointed with our lack of willingness to stop fishing, the young agent walked slowly back to his pickup and drove off. A couple of minutes later I reeled in the biggest shark of the trip. Chris and I celebrated by shotgunning a couple of cold ones. God bless a free America!

CHAPTER ELEVEN

2009 NATIONAL CHAMPIONSHIP GAME: NEVER TRUST A STREET VENDOR WHO SELLS TICKETS

THIS STORY TAKES place back in Orlando, Florida. If you recall, this is where Chris and I were in 2001 for the previous National Championship game between the in-state favorite team, the Florida State Seminoles, and the Oklahoma Sooners. This time, however, the adventure would turn out much differently. This time, the Sooners would not come out on top. The reigning Heisman Trophy winner Tim Tebow and new in-state favorite team, the Florida Gators, would squeak out a narrow, come-from-behind win over the Sooners and their coach, Big Game Bob Stoops.

Like our travel to previous games, Chris and I went to Florida the day before the game, but this time with real airplane tickets, not standby. We spent the night before the game pub crawling and meeting a ton of Gator and Sooner fans. One thing was unanimous: most people, if not everyone, loved Tim Tebow and his leadership. How could you not like a young kid that openly states "God is great and we are all blessed"? Both Chris and I respected the heck out of the guy, but we still wanted him to lose that game. Any other time, place, or opponent, though, we would have rooted for that young man.

On game day, we arrived at the stadium a few hours ahead of the game and sought out ticket brokers and/or common fans offloading additional tickets for a nice profit. We found a few tickets but not a ton. Just a reminder: the Florida Gators were basically playing a home game and didn't have to travel across the country like the Sooner fans, so they snatched up most of the loose tickets. However, Chris and I were batting a thousand in finding tickets over the years. This time would be different. Chris and I split up and started working on different sides of the parking lot and streets. Within twenty minutes or so, Chris found me and said, "Bro, I found two tickets from a reputable ticket broker. They aren't great seats—they're up high—but the price is right." I told him to do the deal so we can go back and focus on drinking and tailgating with our new friends.

A few hours later, we headed to the gates and attempted to enter the gate. As I gave the ticket taker the ticket, they said, "It won't scan. Where did you get this ticket?"

"From a ticket broker," I responded.

"I think this is a fake," the employee said. "Please step out of line before I call security."

I responded in a loud voice, *"Please, I encourage you to call security!"*

The lady immediately radioed for a security officer, who showed up and took Chris and I to the detention area and started the investigation. They asked what company or broker sold the tickets to Chris, and he responded, "Some guy in the parking lot."

The security officer just laughed and said, "You guys were taken advantage of. I'm sorry, but you're not the first ones and will not be the last ones to get scammed. Unfortunately, you will have to leave the premises immediately."

The officer escorted us to the exit gate. We couldn't believe that we had just been scammed for nearly five hundred dollars. What now?

We decided to find an outdoor bar close to the stadium to watch the game. Fortunately, we found a rooftop bar across the street that had seats from which you could see inside the stadium. From that distance, the players looked like ants. It wasn't nearly the same feeling as being at the game in the stadium. Perhaps it was karma after having so many previous miracles of traveling to big games and getting tickets from strangers.

CHAPTER TWELVE

MISSOURI CITY BUFFALO FARM: MISTAKEN IDENTITY

OVER THE YEARS, Chris and I have traveled the world with our families and often by ourselves. We have been blessed to have watched some of the most epic sporting events in some of the greatest American cities. Along the way, we have met some of the nicest and most generous people. Many of the kindest and most respectful people have been first responders and veterans. We both have the utmost respect for these men and women who voluntarily sign up to serve and protect American citizens. That is one thing many people do not understand, especially the younger crowds: unlike many other countries around the world, the United States does not require you to serve. The last time any Americans were drafted was over half a century ago (thank goodness). Many young men and women graduate high school and enlist into a military branch for minimum earnings. They each have their own reasons, but honestly, signing a document saying you will give everything, including your life, for a stranger, is the bravest thing anyone can do for another human being. But this chapter is not about traveling the world, vacationing across the country by the ocean, or even leaving Kansas City to attend a big event. This is a simple trip to a nearby public park surrounded by a large lake and buffalo farm. The farm is also home to a large population of elk and other animals.

Each year, hundreds of thousands of people visit the popular area with their families to take pictures, and if lucky, feed the wild animals through the tall fence. Some people bring apples or carrots, while others simply pick tall grass from around the fences and surrounding fields to feed the animals. The facility has secured deputies on patrol from the county sheriff's department and officers from the fish and game. They randomly patrol the area while working their assigned beat.

On this weekend day, the weather was great, the wives were out shopping, and neither of us had children yet. Chris suggested we pack a cooler of beer, take a drive to the lake, and swing by the buffalo enclosure along the way to see the buffalo and elk. I agreed, so we took off for the lake.

Upon arrival, we found a nice picnic shelter overlooking the lake and cracked open a few cold ones. The afternoon and sun were starting to slip away, so it was time to head back to meet up with the wives for a nice dinner out. The good news is the park was close to our neighborhood (approximately fifteen minutes away). As I pulled out of the pavilion and started toward the house, we passed by the buffalo and elk enclosures. At this time of day there weren't many people to be found. Most of the families had already left to take the kids home for dinner.

About two miles past the enclosure but still located within the park area, I noticed we were being followed by a sheriff's deputy. A few seconds later, the deputy hit the lights and sirens and pulled us over.

I believed the first words from the sheriff's mouth would be, "Have you two been drinking?" Nope. It was actually, "Would both of you step out of the car?"

I was very scared and surprised and said, "Why, and what is going on?"

The deputy said, "I have a report that someone in a car that is the same color as yours was seen shooting at the buffalo thirty minutes ago and actually hit and injured one of the animals."

My exact words were something like "What the f***. . ."

Seconds after both of us said a short prayer under our breath, we heard the deputy's radio blare, "We found them." It was another deputy. "We have two high school kids in custody on the other side of the park. Please report immediately and help me search the car."

We were both thankful we wore our brown pants to the park that day! Too close for anyone's comfort.

CHAPTER THIRTEEN

MIDDLE SCHOOL BASKETBALL TEAM: NOT EVEN CLOSE TO COACH OF THE YEAR

BECAUSE OF SOME unfortunate family matters with my and Raquel's distant relatives, we were thrown into becoming foster parents to a middle-school-aged girl. (For the sake of not causing further embarrassment to her, we'll keep her real name out of this story and call her Alice instead.) At the time, Raquel and I only had one child, a two-year-old son. So, let's just say we were still figuring it out as young parents.

Alice moved to Kansas City during winter break between semesters of her sixth-grade school year. She came from a rural school district that could have fit into one of Kansas City's high schools alone. It was going to take some time to adjust to the size and culture of a large district versus a small country school where she was previously.

We encouraged Alice to get involved in before- and after-school programs and make new friends. Fortunately, she was very outgoing, had a wonderful personality, and was fond of sports as well. Raquel signed her up for the local middle school girls basketball program. It was a club sport, and both Alice and Raquel loved basketball. Raquel had played middle school and high school back in the day, so I assumed that Raquel was going to volunteer to help coach the team. Well, that didn't happen. Raquel, unknowingly to me, signed our foster daughter up and listed me as a volunteer assistant coach. Fortunately, I also played some basketball back in the day, in middle and high school.

One night a couple of weeks later, the home phone rang. It was the division representative from the club, stating that they needed me to be a head coach, as the league had too many seventh- and eighth-grade girls signed up and not enough volunteers. As a matter of fact, the club was combining the grade levels together and called it a middle school division. If I didn't agree to coach Alice along with the other girls, they would not be able to play because of a lack of volunteers. Well, talk about your guilt trips. It worked; I agreed to accept the head coaching position.

The first decision as a new head coach I made was walking across the street and recruiting Chris for the assistant head coach vacancy. Reluctantly, Chris agreed, with some stipulations: I would supply Chris with an ample supply of Bud Light on a regular basis going forward, and in return I would never get kicked out of a game. Done! Keep in mind that "Uncle Chris" was also a basketball player back in the day, so he had game.

Chris and I attended the mandatory preseason coaches' meeting. We got our roster of players, the practice location, and the day of the week for practice that the league provided. A couple of days later, the schedules were published, and the season was due to start two weeks later.

Chris and I took this volunteer coaching gig very seriously and put together a season-long practice agenda equipped with challenging drills to improve all players' skill levels. We would ensure the girls worked hard, learned the rules of the game, and had the skills needed to be successful by the end of the season. Most people would say we took it too seriously. However, when you put two competitive guys together like Chris and I and tell us the scores matter and will be a part of your coaching record, look out. That is a recipe for disaster.

I noticed within a couple of practices that a young girl—we will call her Amy for the sake of this story—was very demanding and took the club basketball team more seriously than even Chris and I. She was the perfect applicant for the title of team captain. Not to mention, somehow she was one of only two eighth graders on the twelve-player roster. I'm not sure who made the rosters, but it seemed like we got the short end of the stick when it came to older players. Nonetheless, Amy was excited and took her promotion very seriously. She helped to ensure the girls were focused and worked hard. Neither Chris nor I ever had to raise our voices toward the players: Amy was always first to take care of it. Not as a bully—it was more like she used strong words of encouragement. It also helped that Amy was the best player, the hardest-working player, and the most competitive player. We didn't know until the games started that she was probably the league's MVP. Talk about finding a four-leaf clover for your first volunteer coaching gig.

The season began, and the team reeled off three consecutive wins. They were taking the practice material and implementing it during the games. Then the team lost their next two games. Things were becoming more challenging. Amy was struggling with a nagging injury and couldn't play at her best, or even at her average. The team didn't have the depth or the eighth-grade experience like those two teams that beat us.

Chris took on the role as the person that needed to motivate the referees to give team Amy all the calls. Chris worked extremely hard and took his position very seriously. When a three-game losing streak seemed possible, Chris decided it was time to show the girls he had their backs. There were a couple of back-to-back questionable calls that went against us. That was it. Chris got into it with the only blind official in the league and then was passionately thrown out of the game and asked to leave the sideline. Apparently, we set a record: first coach ejected that season.

I finished the game without my wingman, and the girls made an unbelievable comeback to win the game on the last shot by you-know-who. This was just the thing needed to motivate the girls. The team turned it around and went on a five-game winning streak. They finished the season 10–2 and headed into the postseason tournament as the second seed.

We knew we could win the league: the team was finally healthy, they were playing together, and the depth issue earlier in the season was no longer present. The girls worked hard and played well together and supported each other. It was an amazing thing to watch develop over the course of a long winter season. The tournament ended with us hoisting the championship trophy! The championship game wasn't even close. Our team won by double digits and set a couple of records along the way. Amy scored more points than any other player, I ended the season with the most technical fouls recorded in modern-day history, and Chris was the most inspiring assistant head coach in the girls' middle school league.

After all that, Chris and I decided over a couple of cold tall boys that we would retire from middle school girls' basketball forever. We modeled the one-and-done theme. Not to mention, Alice moved back with her family after the seventh-grade year ended. It was a win-win-win for everyone.

CHAPTER FOURTEEN

NEWEST RESIDENT ON JADE STREET: I THOUGHT I HEARD YOU SAY WE'RE PREGNANT

T WAS A very cold Midwestern day in March. The Spragues and our family moved into a small neighborhood in a Kansas City suburb. Randomly, it was the same day, at the same time, and we were just across the street from each other. We had never met previously. Both couples were in their twenties and had not started families yet.

The following month was our first official introduction. Chris and I were each outside doing landscaping on our new homes, and Raquel said, "Ron, go over and introduce yourself to our neighbor."

Within days, we would be breaking bread together on a regular occasion, vacationing together, and even joining the same church. It was like God was working a special plan and placing our two families together on our lifelong journey. Three decades later, we have become best friends, and are nearly inseparable. You will hear more about the events of Jade Street later in this book.

In July 1993, the Sprague's hosted a block party. The center stage was in roughly the middle of the block, located in their driveway. Several families from Jade Street attended the event and participated in great BBQ food, hospitality, and a keg of beer—just another night on Jade Street for many young families just starting their married lives together. Raquel had not been feeling well off and on for several days, so before walking across the street to begin the night of festivities, we thought it might be a good idea to do a pregnancy test, just in case. We did not know what to expect. We had never felt the need to purchase one before, and none of our friends had children. We took the test, and nothing happened. We figured we either did it wrong, or we were not pregnant. Perhaps it was a combination of being somewhat hungover from consuming several different hard drinks in the historic Westport district of Kansas City, Missouri the night before.

We headed over to the block party at the Sprague house to enjoy the rest of the evening with no worries. A little later into the evening, Raquel told Carra about the test and that it didn't work. Carra wasn't as easily convinced that it didn't work, so after a few more drinks, songs, and stories, they headed back across the street to our house to inspect the results. The test is 99.99 percent accurate and registered a *positive* result. Both ladies returned to the block party in search of me. Of course, Raquel wanted me to be the first to know I was going to be a new dad. She approached me and said, "I have something I need to tell you."

I was already several hours into a long night of drinking and hanging with the neighbors but could tell by the look on Raquel's face that something serious was about to happen. Raquel said, "You are not going to believe what I just found out."

"Okay," I said, "you're right, so just tell me."

"We're pregnant."

"Hold on, please say that again—who's having a baby?"

"We're having a baby," Raquel said.

My final conscious words were, "I thought I heard you say we're pregnant?"

"Yes, the test confirms we're pregnant. It's 99.9 percent accurate, but I'll schedule an appointment on Monday to confirm with my doctor."

The neighborhood would never be the same. A couple of hours later, Chris and other members of the Jade Street community had to carry me home and put me to bed. I passed out between Chris and Mark's homes from all of the excitement and the day's great news. On Monday it was confirmed, and Raquel and I welcomed our first son into the world the following February to Jade Street.

CHAPTER FIFTEEN

LAKE OF THE OZARKS: WHERE DID THEY COME FROM?

CHRIS AND I took a trip to Lake of the Ozarks, Missouri, with a twofold purpose: a work-related conference for two days, followed by a guys' fishing event the next two days.

The first day of the conference was very impactful. It was a day filled with numerous activities, including four separate classes to discuss everything from operational excellence to financial policy reform to local and state government funding opportunities for new programs.

Members of my organization and I were asked to do a presentation on our alternative fuel project, called "The Largest Alternative Fuel Project in the United States." This project was up for and later won numerous national awards, including project of the year in two categories: (1) operational excellence and (2) green initiative. Twenty years later, this project is still considered by many experts as the largest and most impactful transportation project in the United States for public education.

The day ended with a tremendous amount of excitement surrounding the presentation and networking with many professionals from the same industry. After a group vote, it was decided that everyone would go back to the hotels and get changed from our formal attire to much more relaxing shorts and polos. I also wanted to pick up Chris, who had been attending the conference as a guest. He was essentially awaiting the guys' fishing trip.

With Chris and I, plans always seem to change once alcohol is introduced. This day and event would have those same twists and turns.

The evening began with a happy hour between 5:00 and 6:00 p.m. that included a wine tasting event. I wasn't too excited about this part but, as always, went along to support Chris, who loves all types of wines, beers, and hard liquor. Chris gave his very best and was able to taste every bottle at this local winery and even took all my samples as well. It was a championship effort for sure.

As we left the local winery for our steakhouse reservation at 6:30 p.m., Chris began to get extremely tired. His eyes began to close, so I decided it would be best to take Chris from the restaurant dining room, where he had started his nap with his head firmly placed on the table next to his steak dinner.

After dropping Chris off at the hotel, I went back to the restaurant and finished up my steak dinner and desert. After a great meal, the crew decided to do what guys do: we headed to a dance club. This is a unique club, as only women were allowed to dance on stage, and men were only allowed to watch, cheer them on, and throw or place money if they liked the entertainers.

The women did a great job and were paid well for their two-hour event. It was now time to head back to the hotel.

As the crew left, we noticed the parking lot was overflowing, and there were very tight spaces to get out. It was so tight that our driver unfortunately backed into the neon flashing sign that was there to notify people on the highway to stop by for the event. According to the investigation that was conducted by the area's finest law enforcement officers, the sign broke the bumper loose from our truck. Obviously, we didn't notice this when we pulled out onto the highway. We drove about fifteen minutes back to the hotel. As we pulled off the highway and into the hotel parking lot, I noticed from the front passenger seat flashing lights behind us in the parking lot. I asked, "Why are all those flashing lights behind us in the parking lot, and where did they come from?"

We would soon find out that the first vehicle was an employee of the Missouri State Troopers Association, followed by an employee with the Camden County sheriff's office as well as the Osage Beach local police department. Apparently that fifteen-minute drive got the attention of several people. According to the first officer that approached the passenger window, it was the sparks from dragging the bumper that got everyone's attention. The state trooper began his interrogation by asking the driver to step out of the truck. I noticed that the back windows were rolled down a few inches and along the right side of the truck was the sheriff's deputy watching the remaining four of us in the truck. Along the left side of the truck was the local officer who was doing the same. It was about that time I heard the person in the middle back seat say, "I may have a warrant for outstanding unpaid parking tickets from Springfield, Missouri. If they ask us to step out and provide our driver's license, I'll be making a run for it."

I couldn't believe what I just heard. This was the first time I had met this gentleman, but I quickly realized that he probably wasn't that smart. I also noticed that the sheriff's deputy had also heard the comment and was laughing about what he heard. About that same time, I was asked to provide my driver's license, and when it came back clean, that officer said, "Sir, you are free to leave if this is where you're staying. I suggest you go inside and stay inside the remainder of the night."

"You bet," I said, and I walked straight to my hotel room and didn't look back.

Apparently two of the other members in the truck were not so lucky. They were taken into custody and processed out. The crazy guy that said he was going to make a run for it ended up staying a little longer. What a night!

The next morning when I woke up, I went out to the patio and saw Chris enjoying his morning coffee on the adjacent patio. Chris began to apologize for being overserved and falling asleep before dinner was served in front of my colleagues. I told him there was no need to apologize because half the crew ended up in jail that night. Perhaps his unscheduled nap saved Chris from an extended stay at America's finest law enforcement buildings.

CHAPTER SIXTEEN

VEGAS ALL-NIGHTER: GOLDEN ARM

I T WAS AN amazing trip to famous Las Vegas for the Cox and Sprague families—parents only this time. The original plan was to head to Vegas, stay on the Strip, and perhaps catch a couple of the world-famous shows that only Vegas could offer.

The actual trip was months in the making and vetted over several cocktails and long conversations with the wives, of course. If you knew Carra and Raquel, you would understand who makes all the travel decisions (it isn't Chris or me). After several meetings, the team decided to go cheap on the hotel, as everyone always says, "You won't even be in your room—at least not early or sober." No truer words have ever been spoken; however, we did want to make sure that we didn't get mugged or assaulted to and from the casinos or shows. So, based on the cost of the rooms, and me providing some feedback on my previous two trips to Vegas, the decision was to stay at Circus Circus Hotel and Casino on the Strip. What a hotel. Let's just say it's cheap, located right in the heart of the famous Strip, but that is about it for the highlights of that place.

As we approached the building to our rooms, which was located behind the main building and on the back side of the parking lot, Chris noted that there appeared to be the outline of a body that was chalked on the pavement next to the front door. It was never confirmed if or who was killed in the parking lot.

After unpacking and getting the ladies calmed back down, it was decided to head back to the front part of Circus Circus, walk around, and check out the surroundings. We ended up heading right to the slot machines and table games. We played for a couple of hours and headed off to another Vegas attraction, the Buffet at Luxor.

After dinner we went back to the tables and slot machines. The ladies played until 10:00 p.m. and then decided to hit the hotel room for rest and to be fully prepared for the next two days. Chris and I ended up heading back to the roulette table for a couple of hours. Let's just say lady luck was on our side that night, as we left around midnight with a couple grand in our pockets.

I couldn't get to sleep and decided to head back to the casino floor. I spent the night at the craps and roulette tables. When we all four met the following morning around 7:00 a.m., I had made nearly four grand. For some reason, lady luck was still on my side.

After a long day of sightseeing and shopping, the crew decided to head downtown for dinner and gambling. As the ladies bounced from slot machine to slot machine and table game to table game, Chris and I planted ourselves firmly at a craps table with our new best friend, Mr. Lee. He was a middle-aged Asian man who loved playing craps but would end up loving Chris and I more than craps after a couple of hours (he eventually started referring to himself as our "gay friend"). I got the dice and began to roll and ended up rolling over fifty-four straight rolls, hitting numerous points, both the high and low and everything in between. Our new friend, Mr. Lee, would grab my arm and rub it before every toss of the dice, and he continued to call me the "Golden Arm." As I continued to hit point after point, Mr. Lee continued to double all his bets. After two hours, Mr. Lee was quickly moving up the list of the top ten wealthiest citizens of Las Vegas. Not to mention both Chris and I were well over five thousand dollars.

The trip was a *big* success, and after two days it was entirely paid for. On day three, no one wanted to gamble and lose all our progress (which Vegas is known for). So, we shopped, ate well, and caught our shows. Next time, we thought, we'd stay at Caesars Palace. We could afford it if we just put that money away.

CHAPTER SEVENTEEN

BIG 12 BASKETBALL TOURNAMENT: THAT LINE IS TOO LONG

AS WE HAVE already established in earlier chapters, Chris and I enjoy sports, especially the Big 12. In 2002, we managed to secure tickets to nearly every session of the tournament. The big event was once again in Kansas City, at the historic Kemper Arena down in the "not-so-good" area of the city.

It was a Friday, and the tournament was on day two of the four-day event. Chris and I had already watched the late-morning session and decided to head downstairs from the arena to an old bar called Replays. The old bar wasn't much of a secret. It was small and apparently didn't have a building code capacity. If it did, no one enforced it. The bar was big enough for fifty to seventy-five people, but during tournaments it was stretched to a couple hundred fans. Remember, if you went outside, the choices were limited, and there was a chance you may even get mugged if it was after the late session and you were traveling alone. Another important fact was the limited restrooms. If you have capacity for fifty to seventy-five fans in your bar, two stalls for women and two stalls for men are not going to be enough for two hundred.

Chris and I had invited a guest to join us at the tournament. She happened to be a *big* basketball fan and neighbor. She was a nice person, but she was a University of Kansas graduate, so we had to tolerate her fight song and all the crazy chants. In all seriousness, she was a cool person to hang out with. We invited her because KU was playing during the second session. After several rounds of drinks, she let us know that she was heading to the restroom. About forty-five minutes later, she showed back up and said that the lines were so long that the women were using the men's restroom, so good luck in getting into the men's side if we needed to go. I think that's where the jinx came from. Within ten minutes, I had to take a piss, and I was not going to wait thirty to forty-five minutes. I would end up peeing myself.

Our neighbor had the great idea of taking a banner off the wall and holding it up next to our table to block the view while I took a piss. After a few rounds of drinks, it sounded like a reasonable idea. So, with that advice, I proceeded to remove the KU  banner from the wall, and the neighbor and Chris held it up next to the table while I peed under the table into a large cup that I later threw in a nearby trash can. What a relief! For her effort and idea, I rolled up the banner, placed it down my pants, took it to the arena, and later gave it to the neighbor for a souvenir. We still have no idea how we pulled this stunt off without a single person telling an employee or worse yet contacting security. I guess everyone was as overserved as us.

CHAPTER EIGHTEEN

RED RIVER RIVALRY: BARRY SWITZER MIRACLE

FOR THOSE WHO aren't college football fans, the Red River Rivalry is one of the oldest and typically best college football matchups each year. The game is the highlight of one of the world's largest state fairs, the Texas State Fair.

That year was no different. Nothing else matters on that day other than the final score—throw out the previous games, current records, and updated rosters. Typically, the winner of the game gets to move to the driver's seat for another conference championship. That year we were blessed: earlier in the year I found out that my wife Raquel worked with a great OU connection at her Kansas City office. The outside sales guy was the father-in-law of the assistant OU athletic director. Calling in a couple of favors, I was able to secure fifty-yard-line tickets at the historic Cotton Bowl Stadium. Another little-known fact is the fifty-yard line represents the actual barrier between the OU fans and the Texas fans. Literally at the exact position of the fifty-yard line you will find seat assignment numbered 1 heading east from the 50, and the first seat heading west is also numbered 1. One direction OU, the other Texas. It is an amazing atmosphere to watch a game in.

The game kicked off right on time at 11:00 a.m., and Chris and I were already in our amazing seats located in row 5. Within the first few minutes, I noticed that one of my favorite childhood idols was seated in row 1, a couple seats over: it was none other than Barry Switzer, one of the greatest OU coaches from the '70s and '80s. I turned and challenged Chris to approach Coach Switzer to get both of our hats and game-day programs autographed. Although the tailgate was quality and numerous alcoholic drinks were already flowing on this beautiful Dallas morning, Chris said, "There is no way Barry will sign our programs and hats."

"Have you ever met him before?" I said. "He is always appreciative of OU fans, especially football fans."

In all honesty, Chris has the tendency to be a little more reserved than I am. Looking for another way out, he said, "Dang Ron, I didn't even bring a Sharpie. Sorry brother."

Of course, I wasn't going to let Chris off the hook after the roles were reversed just a few years earlier in Kansas City. At that time, Chris encouraged me to crawl over several rows of seats and get the autograph of the OU men's basketball head coach, Kelvin Sampson, at a Big 12 Tournament. I was able to secure signatures on both hats and programs.

The final straw was me betting Chris all the money in his pocket that not only would Coach Switzer be more than willing to sign, but he would also have a Sharpie in his pocket. With the money now in play, Chris proceeded to climb over a couple of rows of seats and approach the coach. As I watched, Chris shook Coach Switzer's hand, then proceeded to ask for his autograph. Sure enough, just like I had predicted, Coach Switzer reached into his front pocket and pulled out a sharpie and signed all three items before Chris climbed back over the seats. A Dallas morning miracle. Those items are still framed in my man cave.

CHAPTER NINETEEN

ROCKBRIDGE FISHING TRIP: DON'T SHOOT! & WHERE IS ALL THE PATIO FURNITURE?

IT WAS ANOTHER responsible fathers fishing trip. This time the group selected a popular trout farm in southern Missouri on the Arkansas border. It was Chris, two other dads from Lee's Summit, and myself. Chris and I drove separately and agreed to meet the other two at the entrance to the cabin.

The trout farm was kind of off the beaten path by design so that you had a ton of privacy and could just be one with nature, off the grid for a while. The first day, the weather was beautiful and full of fishing and, most importantly, plenty of catching. The coolers were beginning to fill up with trout, so we decided we'd have to drink more beer to make room for day two's fishing. No worries: we were experienced in the art of emptying a cooler.

As the sun began to set on day one, I volunteered to cook hamburgers while the others gathered firewood and built up a nice supply for the two-day adventure. After dinner, we decided to bring out the shotguns and shoot cans, bottles, and whatever else we could find for target practice. As it turns out, this wasn't the best idea. Four competitive guys taking turns trying to hit stationary targets wasn't enough competition. Somehow, one of the four irresponsible dads convinced Chris to hide behind a tree about twenty yards away and throw plastic water bottles out from behind the tree so that the other three could try to hit a moving target. As the idea evolved and the shooting got more and more competitive, the bottles kept flying out from behind the tree faster and faster, like the beer flowing. After twenty minutes or so, Chris took the mature approach of saying, "Gentlemen, I don't think this is the best idea. The tree I'm hiding behind has already been hit twice."

Perhaps this was the best advice we've ever heard from Chris. "Good call," I said. This was a bad idea from the start.

After calling off the target practice, we brought patio chairs to the backyard and circled the firepit while one of the dads started a nice-sized campfire for the evening's drinking and story-time events.

After a couple more hours, Chris, myself, and one of the other gentlemen decided to call it a day and hit the bed for an early morning river trip to catch some more trout. The fourth dad thought it was way too early, so he decided to stay up for a "last round" by himself.

When we woke up, the three early-to-bed dads were present for breakfast and the river trip. Unfortunately, the last dad to bed that night couldn't be woken. He was apparently too over-served the night before. Eager to go fishing, the three decided to leave the cabin and head to the river. As we went around back to gather our fishing poles and get into the truck, we happened to notice that someone had thrown all the patio furniture into the fire pit. There wasn't much left except for a couple of metal parts from the chairs. I couldn't help but think that I booked this place on my credit card and how much that furniture was going to cost me.

Away we went to the river for fishing. It was a very hot day for southern Missouri, so we decided to move to the farthest part of the ranch and find some deeper water under some shade trees. As Chris and I waded into the middle of the river, nearly waist-deep, to fish, the third dad said he would stay closer upstream by the truck, next to the gravel bar and road. Little did Chris and I know that the dad did not bring waders and just stripped down to his boxers and waded a few yards into the river before climbing

onto a rock to fish out into the deeper water of the river. Everything seemed to be working for all three of us, as the trout were biting despite the heat.

About a half hour later, a small, reconditioned school bus pulled down next to the river and parked next to our truck. Within a few minutes, a small group of children climbed out and walked along the trail to the spot on the river where the dad was standing on the rock with nothing but his boxers on. His clothes were still on the riverbank next to where the children were standing. A couple minutes later a preacher showed up and asked what was going on. "Just fishing and trying to stay cool," the dad said.

Apparently, the preacher and families were coming to the river for a baptism event or something. The three of us hurried to gather our belongings so we could leave before anyone got arrested or things got any more awkward. We went to the cabin and revived our friend, then headed back to Kansas City.

CHAPTER TWENTY

ARROWHEAD STADIUM ADVENTURE: WHOSE SUITE IS IT ANYWAY?

I DON'T HAVE TO remind you how much Chris and I and our families love football. This is another one of those football game outings that turned out differently than you might imagine. Again, it always seems to be more than a great game.

This time we were closer to home, at a stadium recently made famous by Andy Reid and Patrick Mahomes, among others. However, this game was not an NFL match but rather a regular season game between KU and OU. It was 2005, and both teams were in the middle of successful seasons. The game was close. OU only scored a single offensive touchdown in the fourth quarter. The other points came on a pick six and two field goals.

That, however, was not the highlight of the event—that would come later.

I had recently been introduced to a Lee's Summit gentleman through some business transactions. Apparently he found out I was a *big* Sooners fan, so he asked me if I wanted to bring some family and friends to the KU versus OU football game the following week at Arrowhead Stadium. Unfortunately, he would be out of town but had several seats available in his Jackson County Sports Commission Suite. Those seats are located on the south side of the stadium at approximately the fifty-yard line. They are premium seats, so of course I told him yes, I would take the eight seats he had. My first call was to Chris and another local football fan from Lee's Summit—let's just call him Nick to avoid any embarrassment. Unfortunately, Nick rooted for KU his entire life, but other than that he was a good friend from church, so what the heck.

Like all football games, there was a lengthy tailgate process, then we went into the game just before kickoff. Everyone was excited and already feeling the effects of several pregame shots. Once inside the suite, Nick and Chris decided to go on a tour of the stadium, starting with the suite next to ours. In that suite was the athletic director of the University of Kansas, sitting there by himself and apparently a couple of security guards.

I'm sure the suite door from the hallway was secured and locked to give the athletic director some privacy, but that didn't deter Chris and Nick: they took a much shorter route. There was a window between the suites that you could slide open. Typically both parties need to agree to open the windows for fresh air. Well, the athletic director apparently needed some fresh air. So, Nick opened our window and proceeded to crawl through with Chris. The AD was somewhat surprised but didn't freak out and was nice. I decided that it was best for me to stay in our suite and observe the conversation.

They spoke to each other for a few minutes. Nick got his picture and a signed program and returned to the appropriate suite. Within thirty minutes, security arrived at our suite and started interrogating everyone. Nick and Chris didn't want to take credit for their adventure. The security asked who was "in charge," so I volunteered, as the tickets were officially in my name. I went outside to the hallway to finish the Q&A session.

"Hold on while I call the president of the Jackson County Sports Complex Authority," I told the security guard. "I'm sure he'll want to straighten this whole mess out before anyone has to leave." I called my contact that left the tickets for me. He let me know that he would call the head of security and the owner of the suite next to ours and this whole thing would get resolved. Within another twenty minutes, the security guards said they had received a call to walk away and leave us alone. I got a call as well, and the Jackson County commissioner let me know he called the owner of the suite, who just happened to be the general manager of the Kansas City Chiefs, and everything was resolved privately between the two of them. Later, I would find out that the commissioner and GM had a heated argument about a proposed stadium funding bill. The commissioner told me that he told the GM he didn't want to go there and disrupt my friend and his family's event and that if he did, there may be consequences. What a mess that was quickly resolved with, once again, cash.

CHAPTER TWENTY-ONE

THE SIDE HUSTLE: THE FAMOUS REPO DUO

OVER THE PAST thirty years, Chris and I have developed an amazing friendship. What is even more amazing is the fact that you can't choose your family, but you can choose your friends, and especially your best friend. Chris and I have been best friends for the better part of thirty years now. We have done and seen nearly everything you can imagine during this time. We have witnessed miracles, and even performed some ourselves, according to the stories told by friends and family.

One thing that can be used to gauge how close you are as friends is to ask someone to help perform your duties, regardless of the risk involved. Well, I think this was the test that Chris used to determine how committed I was to our friendship. It all started over a cold drink on the deck, talking about "the worst part of your job." Chris said he felt one of the worst parts of his job was collecting assets that customers refused to make payments on. This practice is better known as being a "repo man." I agreed that it would suck to have to go to someone's home or place of business to get your collateral back.

I asked Chris, "Are you ever concerned about getting shot for trespassing and taking someone's car?"

In a classic Chris response, he said, "Well, sure."

A couple weeks later, Chris approached me and said, "My friend, I have to go to North Kansas City this weekend and pick up a waterbed that the customer no longer wants and cannot afford the payments on. The lady said she and her boyfriend no longer lived together." Chris asked if I would help, given that I had a pickup and Chris did not. I agreed to do so if it was a voluntary deal and I didn't have to beat anyone up (like the boyfriend, who may show up because Chris only had one side of the story).

Fortunately, the first repo job went off without any problem. Chris and I arrived at the house on Saturday morning and picked up the furniture. This kicked off a series of events that took Chris and I all over the city doing repo work on all kinds of things, from furniture to vehicles. Again, upon graduating college, neither Chris nor I ever believed we would become repo agents. However, like Chris always says, "Twenty bucks is twenty bucks," so we did repo work on the side.

One night changed everything. We were on a stakeout, canvassing a neighborhood in Lee's Summit for a car that Chris had a loan on that the customer refused to pay. Once we located the car, we realized it was parked in the front yard of a rental duplex. The car was pinned in by a pickup truck, and access wouldn't be easy. I dropped Chris off across the street, and as

Chris approached the front yard, someone could be heard yelling, "Get off my property or I will shoot your a**!"

That was the end of the nights-and-weekends job as a repo agent. Chris quickly applied for and found another job at a financial organization that didn't make those types of loans. Everyone in both families was extremely happy! How many friends have become repo agents together?

CHAPTER TWENTY-TWO

RAQUEL'S BIRTHDAY: TOO MANY FISHBOWLS

CHRIS AND I know how to celebrate special occasions. This time, it was to celebrate Raquel's milestone birthday (40th).

In Kansas City, there is no better place to celebrate a special occasion than Power and Light. It is the original destination corridor for entertainment in Kansas City. The area is filled with historic brick buildings. The character of the district is created by numerous small restaurants, comedy clubs, and bars. Rarely do you see a major brand or franchise. Just mom-and-pop businesses filled with people trying to forget a long workweek.

Four couples from Lee's Summit attended this special birthday party. Of course, Raquel took center stage. It was her big night.

We settled in at our favorite hangout spot, Howl at the Moon. Raquel started early in the evening and continued to order fish bowl after fish bowl filled with her favorite sweet, light-blue liquor. In all honesty, it tasted quite a bit like blue Kool-Aid. Everyone seemed to enjoy themselves and, more importantly, the fish bowls. They just kept coming.

As the ladies in the group continued to drink their newly found liquid courage, they were summoned by the DJ to the stage to perform their best versions of the 1980s rock-and-roll songs. As the karaoke competition continued, it was clear the winner was Raquel and her version of "You Shook Me All Night Long." Of course, the winner received free drinks, the perfect gift for a woman celebrating her 40th birthday.

Eventually, the ladies tapped out first and converted to water to avoid passing out and throwing up. However, this was the furthest thing from the minds of Chris and I. We kept a steady pace for another couple of hours, until Chris looked over at me and noticed I was "struggling" and had a hard time keeping my eyes open. I've always understood that Kool-Aid packed a punch with a sugar high, but I had no idea it would contain enough alcohol to knock me out.

Within seconds, Chris said, "Down goes Ron." My eyes rolled back and I fell backwards off the barstool, hitting the raised area of the floor. In that part of the restaurant, people had tables and chairs that were raised up a foot or so next to the stage. Everyone just gasped and thought I broke my neck, cut open my head, or worse. However, with catlike reflexes, I gathered myself and stood up. It's another miracle: apparently it just happened to be enough force to wake me up from his four-hour drink festival. Not to miss a beat, Chris proceeded to order another fishbowl and the crew closed the bar at 2:00 a.m. On the way home, I said, "I think that is the hardest I've ever gotten hit, even playing football for a few years." From a broken neck to just another wake-up call. It's safe to say that the sweeter the alcoholic beverage, the more dangerous it can be. What a night in the Power and Light District.

After we closed out the Power and Light we decided to head back toward our hometown; however, we were all needing to find some grub. We couldn't think of a better place than a twenty-four-hour Denny's in Independence, Missouri. Thank goodness for our "sober driver" pledge that Raquel's friend, Vicki, committed to well in advance of the birthday party. She agreed that we needed to find some food for Raquel and the rest of the tribe. As we settled into the all-night restaurant, we quickly began to order nearly everything on the menu that said "all you can eat." Both Chris and I settled in with a new personal best at twelve pancakes in ninety minutes. This didn't include the side orders of bacon, eggs, and some occasional sausage we took from others' plates.

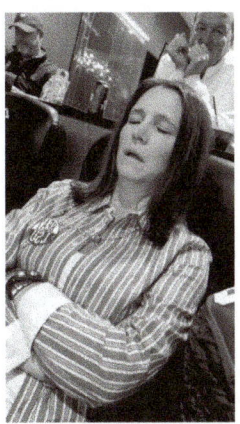

CHAPTER TWENTY-THREE

OKLAHOMA CITY: I LOVE SOCCER

DESPITE THE OVERALL popularity of the NFL, MLB, or let's not forget about the stable NBA, one of the fastest-growing sports in the world continues to be soccer. The MLS organization continues to grow in the United States each year adding teams throughout the country. I am a former soccer coach, and I coached for nearly twenty years before retiring in 2017. My last stop was the Real Madrid club in Madrid, Spain. I and two other coaches had the opportunity to take five high school players from the Kansas City area to train with the Real Madrid Youth Academy, which was a once-in-a-lifetime experience for me. It was also an unforgettable moment for the players and their families.

However, this story isn't about that trip. This chapter is about the passion that I have for soccer, especially the US national team as they tried to win a World Cup. Chris would experience this passion on a business development trip to Oklahoma City with me.

Chris and I traveled to Oklahoma City to connect with an organization which I was doing consulting work on a commercial construction project. Chris and I ended up booking a hotel room in Bricktown, in downtown Oklahoma City. Chris spent the day working remotely and pub crawling in the afternoon. I attended the meeting held at the construction site just outside of OKC in the smaller community of El Reno, Oklahoma. After the meeting, at around 5:00 p.m., I returned to downtown OKC with the contractor and other consultants on the development team. After a quick shower and change of clothes, we decided to head over to a nice restaurant called Mickey Mantle's in the downtown area.

The crew started the dinner with a couple of cold drinks, then went on to some of the biggest and best steaks Chris and I have ever had. After dinner was over, we went into a cigar room in the restaurant for a couple of cigars and a celebration. The good news was that the meeting with the city, contractor, and developer went very well that day, and everyone was feeling great about the outcome. After another hour, the crew asked for the check, and when it arrived, the owner of the company from El Reno was overwhelmed with the amount. It wasn't hundreds of dollars: it was four figures. He seemed so shocked that I asked, "Do you need us to pass a hat and ask for donations?"

The owner responded, "No, I'm just shocked at the amount." I should mention that Chris and I had traveled to OKC at the owner's request as a "favor" and didn't even charge consulting fees, so we thought it was worth it.

We weren't quite finished for the day, so we decided to hit a local sports bar as we walked back to the hotel. I mentioned that I wanted to watch the US national team play in the World Cup game that night that was on television. The owner was also a soccer fan, so he said, "Yes, let's stop in and watch the second half before we hit the hotel. I'll buy us a round of drinks."

That turned into an unforgettable moment. As we approached the bar, we couldn't help but notice that there were more Hispanic fans than American fans gathered in the restaurant. In case you didn't know, there are a ton of Hispanic soccer fans that do not like Team USA. Occasionally they may root for them, but never if they're playing the Mexican national team. Fortunately for us, the two teams were not playing each other that night. I started talking to everyone and asking why they were screaming for Team USA to lose, and they said it was because they did not want to see them advance from that pool of teams and potentially have to play team Mexico in the next round.

As the conversation went on, I began to sell them on the team, and eventually turned to the owner of the El Reno company and said, "I bet I can get everyone in this bar, including the Hispanic fans, to chant 'USA, USA, USA.'" Keep in mind that the owner and I had been drinking all evening long, so we were equally confident in our bet. We decided on the bet: if I got everyone in the bar to stand up on their chairs and chant USA, the owner would have to buy everyone in the bar a shot. Deal!

I went to the front of the bar and stood up on a barstool and said, "On three I need everyone to stand up and chant 'USA,' and everyone will get a free shot. Brilliant! One, two, three, let's go." The entire bar stood up on their chairs and chanted "USA" a minimum of three to four times. The owner

thought the Mickey Mantle's bar tab was too much. He just about doubled that amount in one bet. God bless the USA!

CHAPTER TWENTY-FOUR

THE OMNI HOTEL IN DALLAS: THE GREATEST AUDIBLE

TURNING FIFTY-FIVE IS a big milestone. That is the background of this chapter. It was Raquel's 55th birthday, so I wanted to do something above and beyond to exceed Raquel's expectations. The plan was to take her to one of her favorite places on the planet: Hilton Head Island, South Carolina. Raquel's actual birthday is September 1st, so in 2023, I booked a nice Vrbo home a couple of lots away from the ocean. Raquel didn't know at the time that I had secretly invited our two boys and best friends, Chris and Carra, to make this a memorable surprise party.

The entire event was supposed to last a week. When Raquel and I arrived on the island, my son Derek, his fiancée Courtney, and Chris and Carra were already at the beach house . Unfortunately, our youngest son, Kameron, was experiencing flight delays, so he missed the initial surprise. Kameron and his surprise would come later in the evening.

As Raquel and I drove down the street and approached the house, Raquel's first words were, "You have got to be kidding me. You rented this monster house for the two of us." What you need to know is Raquel is very conservative, so she was starting to think, "What a waste of good, hard-earned money."

As we opened the front door and walked in, the surprise of Chris, Carra, Derek, and Courtney unfolded. Raquel was so surprised and probably relieved that someone else would be filling up the house.

Later that day, the crew decided to have a nice romantic dinner at a restaurant on the beach. We went early and had just sat down for pre-dinner drinks. After a couple of drinks, a waiter approached the table from behind Raquel and asked, "Can I refill your waters?" It was actually Kameron. He was able to catch another flight and make it just in time for a second drink and dinner. The day ended on a bright note, as everyone had safe travel mercies.

Day two was another special one. The gentlemen played a round of golf at one of the nicest courses in the United States while the ladies got to kayak with the dolphins and create a once-in-a-lifetime memory for the family. Not to mention, the weather was amazing.

Speaking of the weather, day three wasn't the same. The local forecast stated that an offshore hurricane had turned direction and was heading toward South Carolina, specifically Hilton Head Island. As you can imagine, that news was shocking and forced us to make some decisions: stay and be stuck on the island in storm surge for days without power, or leave two days early and cut the 55th birthday party short. Chris and I began to call around and get feedback from locals. We quickly found out that the Hilton Head airport was closing that day, and nobody would be getting out for days. The local rental car companies were closing, and the owner of the Vrbo left a message saying to please bring in all the outdoor patio furniture and secure everything else.

Well, that was enough bad news. So, I called around and found plane tickets for everyone to fly out of Savannah, Georgia, about an hour away, that day. We also found a hotel outside of the storm area in Dallas, Texas. Plan B was starting to come together. We headed off to Savannah and caught a flight to Dallas. Days four and five were awaiting us at the Omni Hotel located in downtown Dallas, which was amazing. It had a few wonderful restaurants and a rooftop pool with a swim-up bar. Perhaps the most important thing is that we were all together safely and the weather was amazing!

That night, I secured a reservation at one of the two restaurants on the property. It was an upgraded sports bar with plenty of drinks on the menu. As we finished up our dinner, a young, muscular man walked up to me, grabbed my arm, and repeatedly asked me, "Do you know my family?"

I wasn't sure what to say, so I jokingly said, "Yes, do you know mine?"

As the young man began to get more aggressive, I laughed and asked him, "Do you know who I am?" The man wasn't sure how to respond and eventually let go of my arm and walked toward the bar located in the front of the restaurant. A couple of minutes later, the local Dallas police showed up with hotel security and escorted the man outside of the restaurant and started to interrogate him. It took six people to escort the man outside and encourage him to leave. Apparently, the man had mixed some pharmacy-grade meds with some alcohol and had a bad reaction. What a crazy end to day three. Who knew what day four would bring the crew.

Day four started on the rooftop pool with some drinks while Raquel and Carra took a downtown tour of a museum and local attractions. After about four to five hours of drinks at the poolside bar, Chris and I knew pretty much everyone, including the staff. We began to purchase drinks, including shots, for everyone in attendance. As everyone continued to get over-served, the ladies finally showed up to save the day. Raquel, the birthday girl, arrived back in time for some pool time and a couple of drinks before we all had to go get ready for dinner at the hotel's world-famous steak house. To this day, we are still not sure how Chris and I made it to the room and then to the restaurant. We were both already overserved and speaking five different languages.

The restaurant was amazing. The staff found Raquel and our group a special table for the big party. Believe it or not, we started off by ordering more drinks. A couple of minutes after the first round showed up, Chris accidentally knocked over his wine glass and it broke. So that people wouldn't get upset with Chris, my best friend, I proceeded to take my wine glass and toss it over my shoulder. As it hit the ground it broke apart just like Chris's. Staff approached and couldn't quite figure out what had happened. I explained that "it slipped," so the staff went and got more glasses and another round of drinks. What a close call!

I then got up and walked back to the kitchen to ask for the chef. The chef came over and introduced himself. I asked him what his favorite thing on the menu was. He indicated that it was the wagyu steak. When our waiter came around and took our order, I asked what he suggested. He said the eight-ounce wagyu steak. I told him that was perfect: "I'll take the ten ounces."

Apparently, I ate too much, so Derek had to escort me back to the hotel room early so that I didn't get sick. Everyone else finished their wonderful birthday meals and drinks and called it day four. No one got kicked out, no one got sick, and everyone seemed to have a great day. To this day, we still can't figure out how we managed to drink two thousand dollars' worth of drinks at that poolside bar!

CHAPTER TWENTY-FIVE

THE OCTOBER GHOSTING EVENT: THE BASEBALL BAT

IT WAS AN average October night. Our family was participating in a time-honored tradition of "ghosting" players on the youth soccer team, where Chris and I each had a son playing. Back in the day, ghosting was somewhat a random act of kindness.

My family and another youth player from the roster decided to create a bag of treats for each player on the team. The boys made ten bags to be delivered and kept a bag for themselves. Once the bags were completed, off we went to start delivering them throughout the evening to the players' homes. The process involved my son and the other player on the team ringing the doorbell or knocking on the other players' doors, then placing the bags and running away so no one would find out where the treat bag came from.

The team had players all around the community of eighty thousand people, so they were spread from one side of town to the other. This event would take a couple of hours to hit all ten homes. About an hour into the activity, we approached Chris's house. We knew from the years of friendship that Chris and his family would be in the basement of their house watching their traditional Saturday night movies with their two kids. So, the plan was for my son and his teammate to hop the fence in the backyard next to the street and approach the house.

The good news is that Chris and his family lived in a two-story house with a walkout basement. The walkout basement had a sliding glass door that faced the street and made it easier to knock and run quickly to escape capture to our nearby car waiting in the street. The two boys pulled it off to perfection. They hopped the fence, quickly approached the glass door, knocked hard, and ran like crazy. What we didn't know was that Chris and his family were watching a Halloween movie, and the timing of the knock coincided with a very scary part of the movie. Chris, who was located the closest to the glass door, jumped so hard he fell out of the chair. His wife and kids jumped over and behind the sofa for protection from the noise. Chris ran upstairs and got a baseball bat, then snuck outside, from the front of the garage around back, hoping to catch the "bad guy" who he felt was trying to break into his house.

A couple of days later, when Chris and I brought our families together for dinner, Chris said, "You're not going to believe what happened this weekend."

"What are you talking about?" I responded.

Chris said over the weekend, someone tried to break in through his basement door. He told everyone about the scary movie and the baseball bat, and he said he stayed up until 2:00 a.m. sitting in a lawn chair with the bat, awaiting the return of the bad guy.

He said it wasn't until the next day that he actually looked around and found the bag of treats and note that had fallen between the two patio chairs when the boys ran off. I didn't have the heart to tell Chris my family was behind the entire thing until the following weekend, when I confessed over a couple of cocktails. This is still one of the funniest stories shared.

CHAPTER TWENTY-SIX

PIG ROAST ON JADE: SLEEP WITH ONE EYE OPEN

AS WE ALREADY discussed, Chris and I and our spouses randomly met briefly in March 1993, when we just happened to be moving into the same neighborhood, on the same street, on the same snowy day. We formally met the following month in April, when my wife said, "You need to go across the street and introduce yourself to our new neighbors." It just so happened that both Chris and I were outside working to establish our new lawns. Of course, I followed Raquel's advice, and away I went with a cold beer in hand. Over the following thirty years, the two couples became best friends.

In 1993, both couples had some getting-to-know-your -new-neighbors events. These events included numerous activities, such as block parties, where the entire block of Jade Street would be closed off by barricades and live bands were brought in to have a large concert in the street or on someone's driveway. Over the years, the parties seemed to get larger, and neighbors started inviting friends and families. Several times, the fire department stopped by with large pumper trucks or ambulances so the neighborhood children could be introduced to our first responders and check out their cool vehicles.

One specific occasion comes to mind that really forced the neighborhood social committee to revisit their process and policies. Our subdivision didn't have an HOA, and the neighborhood committee was composed of two individuals: Chris and I. We had the power to make all decisions, and no one had veto power. Ok, that may be an overstatement. We all know Carra and Raquel could influence the decisions on occasion. However, Carra and Raquel were also known to go to bed early and leave Chris and I unsupervised from time to time. Especially after midnight. This is precisely what happened this time.

The band was done playing, the crowd dispersed, and the drinks were all consumed, so Chris and I were left alone to finish the cleanup and have "one last drink." Seems like a simple task, but it was Chris and I after an all-day drinking event. The theme for that year's party was a luau. I had picked up a fully roasted hog from a farm that was known to have the best BBQ in the county. It was so good that the entire neighborhood was fed, and nothing was left except the head and some bones. We decided it would be funny to welcome the newest members to the Jade Street neighborhood block party by taking the leftover head from the pig and placing it on a handle we removed from a shovel. We then proceeded to place it firmly in the ground in the front yard of the new neighbor's house.

That didn't go so well the next morning when that family and their two small children got up early to head to church. Apparently, their little children "freaked out" and started screaming and crying for the pig. The neighbors returned from church and took the head on the stick over to Chris's yard and placed it on the driveway. They were so upset they ended up moving out a few weeks later. We still wonder to this day if their children ever recovered?

CHAPTER TWENTY-SEVEN

MOVIE NIGHT AT RON AND RAQUEL'S: FACES OF DEATH

ARLY IN OUR friendship, I asked Chris if he and his wife would be interested in coming over sometime to have dinner and some drinks. Chris said he would check with the wifey and get back to me the following week. After getting our social calendar worked out, we made plans to hang out a couple Saturdays later at our house.

It was a late afternoon, so we hung out on the patio at our house. After dinner, a couple of hours later, we decided the night was still young, so I popped in a recently rented VHS tape from Blockbuster. The movie happened to be an "oldie but goodie"a series called *Faces of Death*. I don't want to ruin the surprise for anyone; however, the series is about people doing crazy things that you would never imagine. Some of the rituals are so ridiculous they aren't even legal in the United States. This series had an episode about humans taking monkeys from the forest and securing them in the center of a small table, with only their heads hanging out above the table. The humans would take a small hammer and hit the monkeys to knock them out, and then the humans would proceed to crack open their skulls with small tools before eating the monkey brains with knives and forks. It was some of the craziest things we had ever witnessed. It was so disturbing that the neighbor couple didn't want to finish watching it. Both women were physically sick to their stomachs.

Chris looked over at me and said, "Hey neighbor, it's getting late. Wifey and I need to get up early to head to church. We better get going." It was obvious the movie selection wasn't the best for either couple. I think Chris and Carra were still trying to figure out if Raquel and I were closet cannibals. If so, they would have cut ties, and the friendship would've been forever over. It was probably a couple weeks before Chris and I ran into each other again. After a couple minutes and a few beers later, Chris found out that I was as freaked out as him and that Raquel was so embarrassed she wouldn't dare approach Carra. Chris said, "Thank goodness, we thought you two were (*&^^%$ crazy!" Chris and I made plans to get the ladies back together the following weekend for a night out on the town. No more first-time rentals with the families!

CHAPTER TWENTY-EIGHT

FAMILY VACATION TO MINNESOTA: THE FLAT TIRE

AS CHRIS, MYSELF, and our families grew closer, we decided one evening over a case of beer that it was time to take our friendship to an all-time high. Raquel and I invited Chris and Carra to go to Minnesota to spend a long weekend at Raquel's historic family cabin on Lake Superior in Minnesota. The cabin is an amazing place, located on the lakeshore, with picturesque views from windows all along the side of the cabin. The property has been in the family for several generations.

Keep in mind, our two families are best described as city slickers. We did not camp much and had never traveled that far as families. I secured a utility trailer from a colleague. Working together for a couple of days, the two families managed to pack nearly everything they could think of on the small trailer, including my small two-person boat. The plan was to leave early in the morning and reach Minneapolis, Minnesota, in the afternoon for some shopping at the Mall of America and a nice dinner.

Typically, things would go much better for others, but not these two families. As we've seen in the last twenty-seven chapters, nothing is easy or simple. This adventure would be no different. Within two hours into this monster voyage, the utility trailer experienced a blowout. So, along the I-35 highway, in the dark, Chris and I turned into a NASCAR pit crew trying to get the tire repaired and off the shoulder of the highway as quickly as possible. What seemed like hours probably only took thirty minutes, and the job was complete. However, with ten more hours and four days in front of us, there was mounting concern that our only spare tire was now in use. We decided when we reached civilization later that day that we would purchase a new tire and retire the spare again for the remainder of the trip. That plan was executed when we reached Minneapolis.

Between the roadside repair and Minneapolis, my mobile phone rang. It was our neighbors back in Kansas City. They said, "I thought you were going on a weeklong vacation this morning?"

I responded, "You bet. Why do you ask?"

"We noticed your garage door has been open for the past six hours. Do you want me to close it?" Apparently, we left so quickly no one thought of closing the doors.

After checking into the hotel and heading to the Mall of America for some shopping by the ladies, the gentlemen headed to a local watering hole for a drink. Then the crew headed to dinner. Somehow, Chris and I got overserved between the two events. At the restaurant, Raquel ordered and told the waiter, "I do not want tomatoes. I can't eat them."

The order showed up with tomatoes on it. Carra was first to speak up and tell the waiter, "My friend is allergic to tomatoes." The waiter responded with a not-my-problem look, so I headed for the swinging doors to the kitchen. As I opened the doors, I tossed the food in the direction of the chef and said, "No tomatoes on this order."

The manager approached the table and asked, "Do you have a problem?"

I took the opportunity to say, "I think we have a language barrier or communication problem between the server and the chef." Believe it or not, the manager was very professional and said he was sorry and would take care of it. When the correct order showed up, Raquel was terrified that they did something bad to it, so she asked for a bag, and we took it to go. Once outside the restaurant she gave it to a homeless person, and we hit a drive-through for her on the way back to the hotel. Just another vacation with the Cox and Sprague families.

CHAPTER TWENTY-NINE

HILTON HEAD ISLAND: WHERE IS THAT PHONE AGAIN?

AS I PREVIOUSLY reported, Hilton Head Island is one of the greatest vacation destinations in the world according to both the Cox and Sprague families. So many quality memories were born on the small island in South Carolina.

Our families have invited several friends and other family members over the years, but one of the best memories of the island involved a trip with us and an elected official from Missouri, who we'll call John, and his wife and children. We decided to tack on two additional days on the front end of the trip to "warm up." We rented three suites at a Hilton resort on the other side of the island. On day one, John hit it early and hard upon our arrival. Both Chris and I wondered, "How is he going to make it to dinner?" Turns out our hunch was correct. John was beyond repair by 5:00 p.m. He remained behind while the rest of us went to dinner at a nice restaurant located on the resort property. When we returned, everyone had the pleasure of watching John throw up his organs over the balcony of the eighth floor. The good news was there weren't people or a pool below, just some grass and a couple of medium-sized trees.

On the morning of day two, I was on the balcony and asked everyone to come out and look at the large flock of birds that were apparently enjoying a nice breakfast amongst all the trees. They seemed to really be enjoying the contents of John's stomach from the night before. To this day, I'm not sure if we ever witnessed that many birds in one flock.

After feeding the birds and checking out on day three, the crew headed to the Vrbo home on the beach on the other side of the island.

We all settled in a beautiful home on Grey Widgeon, which was a second-tier lot away from the ocean. Both the Cox family and Spragues decided to prepare a cooler for the day at the beach. Of course, it was overflowing with Tito's, as that was the go-to for both families. After a morning of Bloody Marys, the crew decided to head back home for lunch. After a couple-hour midday break, the crew headed back to the ocean only to realize the tide changed significantly on that small island. The good news about staying on a private area of the beach on the island is that no one will crowd you out. The bad news is that no one is around to help pull your stuff back away from the rising tide. Luckily, we were able to rescue our chairs and beach equipment. However, our towels were wet, and we probably lost a couple of balls. Not too bad for a valuable lesson in ocean tides. By 3:00 p.m., Raquel was the first victim of the fourth day. She proceeded to pass out on the beach. The good news was that she was under an umbrella, and everyone could keep an eye on her. Unlike John, Raquel covered up the contents of her stomach with sand so no one would step in it and so it wouldn't become a meal for the birds. I carried Raquel back to the house over my shoulder.

By sundown on day five, it was my turn. I decided to take a bike ride into the ocean, attempting to catch up with a shrimp boat that was half a mile away from the shore. I peddled into the ocean with the water up to my chest; however, the boat made a clean getaway, and I was eventually pulled from the bike by the ocean. I ended up losing half the stuff in my pocket, including my iPhone. Chris relayed that it was an amazing thing to watch.

After I was rescued, we decided to chill out in the backyard by the pool before starting up the grill. Chris asked me to bring out some beers from the kitchen to the poolside. As I took off to get the beers for everyone, I slipped on the slick concrete between the hot tub and the pool. I literally went horizontal like Superman and landed on my side. My ribs hit first, and I slid into the hot tub. Thank goodness it wasn't my head. Chris sprung into action and pulled me out. I was still trying to figure out what happened, so they decided to discuss it during another drink and eventually got the grill going. What an epic vacation.

CHAPTER THIRTY

HUNTINGTON BEACH: YOU THOUGHT YOU COULD DANCE

T'S ONLY APPROPRIATE to end the first edition of *Me and My Best Friend* with a recent 2023 story. This will kick off our second-edition book, still in the making, one story at a time.

We needed to make 2023 a major milestone with special events scheduled all year long. We had many things to celebrate. Carra was coming off a year cancer free, Raquel was going to hit the magical double nickel, and Ron was preparing for his fall retirement. We could go on and on.

The first big event was in March 2023. We decided to go back to one of our go-to places, Huntington Beach, California. We arrived two days before my birthday and the day before St. Pat's Day. Two major events and reasons to celebrate the month of March. We found an amazing hotel/resort in the downtown area next to the famous pier.

This trip was a little different because it was only the four of us: Chris, Carra, Raquel and me. No other friends, neighbors, or kids. So, we knew it had the potential to get somewhat crazier than a normal trip. Day one included a daylong adventure at the beach with chairs, umbrellas, and too many drinks to track. We hit it hard and wanted to get back to the resort somewhat earlier than normal so that we could hit St. Pat's Day and my birthday hard the next day.

Day two, March 17th, was an amazing time. The ladies worked hard to make sure they hit every woman's boutique in the central business district while Chris and I tried to match that commitment by hitting each of the downtown bars. The women eventually won. Although Chris and I are professional drinkers, we cannot even compare to the years of experience Carra brings to the women's team. By definition, she is world-class and ranks in the top ten in every shopping category.

The game plan was to shop all day, drink all day, and get back together for dinner at HQ Gastropub, one of our favorite Huntington Beach hangouts. We all made it to HQ Gastropub on schedule. We began ordering green beer towers and our favorite shots. It didn't take long before the group was feeling bulletproof. So, we decided to get up in front of everyone in the pub and start having a dance off. Carra and Raquel are great dancers, but Chris and I were not given that skill. However, with that many green beer towers, we didn't care. You know it's going well when everyone in the pub decides to join the competition or film it so those who couldn't witness it live could stream it on social media. Who knew we would become so popular. A couple of minutes later, Carra tapped out. Not sure exactly what happened—a pulled muscle, being overserved, or pride—but she bailed. Not quite the same as ghosting, but she did leave before the stroke of midnight. In the past, the crew has always tried to make it past midnight so they would be first to wish me a happy birthday at 12:01 a.m. on my actual birthday. Carra was out by 9:00 p.m. The night was still young, so the remaining crew members voted to go to another pub.

We landed back downtown and switched from beer towers to hard liquor. This would prove to be another tactical error. We were partying on the front patio of a local pub. I was an easy target for vendors selling their wares. One lady kept coming up to us and asking me the same question: "Do you want to buy your pretty wife a rose?"

After being approached a few times (who knows, she may have had amnesia), I was getting distracted and said, "How much for the entire cart with all the roses?" She gave me a price and I told her, "I'll take them all if you go home and go to bed." The deal was sealed, and I was the new owner of a cart full of roses. Raquel took over the operations and began to walk through the

pub giving our free roses to all the nice women. We had no idea Raquel would be the next one to tap out, but shortly after passing out all of the roses, she was exhausted and decided to call it night. To her credit, she was doing great at keeping up with Chris and me.

It was now after 10:30 p.m., but still too early for Chris and I, so we ordered a few more rounds for our newly found friends and eventually made it to midnight. Chris hosted a nice long toast to his best friend, me. It was a fantastic way to end St. Pat's Day 2023 and bring in my birthday. Not only were all the guys happy that Chris bought everyone a shot, but the women were also all happy because Raquel gave everyone in the pub a rose. That is the true definition of win-win.

SPECIAL THANKS

I want to say "thank you" to my best friend and major contributor to this book, Chris Sprague. His continued encouragement and commitment to having FUN is the foundation of this book.

LAST WORD

Love deep, laugh more (especially at yourself). Never take yourself too seriously. Perhaps most importantly, give yourself a break.

Live like you're dying. In reality, we all are, my friends!

ACKNOWLEDGMENTS

I want to express my deepest gratitude to our closest friends and my amazing wife, whose love and devotion continually inspire me to do better and be better. Your unwavering support has been crucial in making this dream a reality. You are my Rock!

My sincere thanks go to:

Raquel Cox for her personal editing touch.

Will Latimer for professional images and video production.

Emily Shanholtzer for professional images and video production.

Noah Zak for his professional touch in making me look and sound better.

Each of you has played an essential role in bringing this book to life. Thank you for your dedication and expertise.

AUTHOR BIO

Ron Cox is a thought leader, lifelong learner, and Hall of Fame coach with a passion for professional development and entrepreneurship. With over three decades of experience, Ron has made significant contributions in various fields, including education, transportation, and business leadership.

Ron resides with Raquel, his wife of thirty-three years, and is a proud father to Derek and Kameron. His diverse experiences and commitment to excellence continue to inspire his work and writing.